MACMILLAN ACADEMIC SKILLS

D0491571

Skillful
Reading&Writing

Student's Book

4

Authors: Mike Boyle & Lindsay Warwick
Series Consultant: Dorothy E. Zemach

Contents

🇬🇧 = features British English; 🇺🇸 = features American English

To the Student

Academic success requires so much more than memorizing facts. It takes skills. This means that a successful student can both learn and think critically.

Skillful gives you:

- Skills for learning about a wide variety of topics from different angles and from different academic areas
- Skills you need to succeed when reading and listening to these texts
- Skills you need to succeed when writing for and speaking to different audiences
- Skills for critically examining the issues presented by a speaker or a writer
- Study skills for learning and remembering the English language and important information.

To successfully use this book, use these strategies:

- **Come to class prepared to learn.** This means that you should show up well fed, well rested, and prepared with the proper materials (paper, pen, textbook, completed homework, and so on).
- **Ask questions and interact.** Learning a language is not passive. You need to actively participate. Help your classmates, and let them help you. It is easier to learn a language with other people.
- **Practice.** Do each exercise a few times, with different partners. Memorize and use new language. Use the *Skillful* Digibook to develop the skills presented in the Student's Book. Complete the additional activities on your computer outside of class to make even more progress.
- **Review your work.** Look over the skills, grammar, and vocabulary from previous units. Study a little bit each day, not just before tests.
- **Be an independent learner, too.** Look for opportunities to study and practice English outside of class, such as reading for pleasure and using the Internet in English. Find and then share information about the different unit topics with your classmates.

Remember that learning skills, like learning a language, takes time and practice. Be patient with yourself, but do not forget to set goals. Check your progress and be proud of your success!

I hope you enjoy using *Skillful*!

Dorothy E. Zemach
Series Consultant

Welcome to *Skillful*!

Each *Skillful* unit has ten pages and is divided into two main sections: reading skills and writing skills.

Reading

The reading skills section always comes first and starts with a *Discussion point* to lead you in to the unit topic.

There are then two reading texts for you to practice your reading skills on. There are activities to practice your global reading skills and your close reading skills, as well as opportunities to critically examine the ideas in the texts. Key academic vocabulary from the text is presented on the page so you can see essential terms to learn.

Vocabulary skills also give you the chance to develop the ways in which you learn and remember vocabulary from the reading texts.

Writing

The writing section has two main parts: grammar and writing skills. You can find information on each of these in boxes on the page, and these give essential information on these skills. At the end of this section is a writing task for you to put the ideas from the texts and the skills from the writing section into practice. Use the checklist on page 109 to see how well your partner has completed the task.

The final page in the unit focuses on study skills featuring engaging scenarios which will help you to achieve academic success. Some of these pages come from *Critical Thinking Skills* by Stella Cottrell.

Using *Skillful* gives you everything you need for academic success.

Good luck!

Introduction

Each *Skillful* Student's Book comes with a code in the back of the book that gives you free access to the accompanying Digibook. The Digibook encourages a more interactive and engaging learning environment and is very simple to access. Just go to www.skillfuldigibooks.com, and follow the step-by-step instructions to get started!

The first time you access the Digibook you will need an Internet connection, but after this it is possible to work offline if you wish.

Digibook

This contains all the same content as your printed Student's Book, but you can use it on your computer, enabling easier navigation through the pages, a zoom function to create better student focus, and a personal annotation resource for helpful classroom notes.

Skillful Practice

You can either complete the extra activities as you go through the Digibook via the interactive icons, or you can find them all in one place in the *Skillful* Practice area. Here you will find a variety of activities to practice all the new skills and language you have learned in the Student's Book, including vocabulary, grammar, and skills-based activities.

There are also additional productive tasks and video activities linked to the unit topics.

If you complete any of the extra activities while you are online, your score will be recorded in your markbook so that your teacher can track your progress. If you work offline, your scores will be stored and transferred to your markbook the next time you connect.

Whether online or offline, in the classroom or on the move, the *Skillful* Digibook allows you to access and use its content while encouraging interactive learning and effortless self-study.

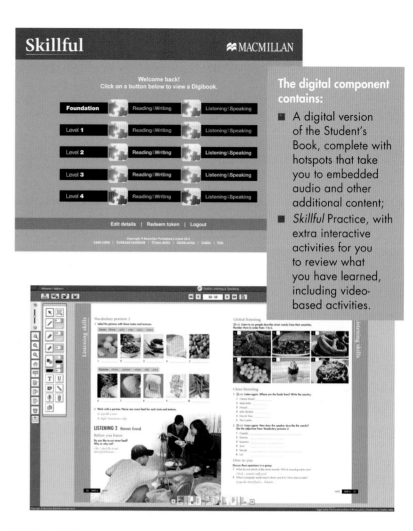

The digital component contains:

- A digital version of the Student's Book, complete with hotspots that take you to embedded audio and other additional content;
- *Skillful* Practice, with extra interactive activities for you to review what you have learned, including video-based activities.

The Digibook also contains lots of hotspots that link to additional content not in your printed Student's Book:

- Audio files for all of the reading texts
- Useful language to support discussion activities
- Dictionary definitions for the *Academic Keywords*
- Unit checklists so you can monitor how well you are progressing through the course.

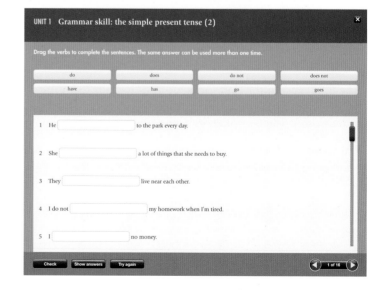

Gathering

READING	Identifying the writer's position
CRITICAL THINKING	What exactly is an argument?
LANGUAGE DEVELOPMENT	Synonyms
	Simple and progressive verb forms
WRITING	Formality

Discussion point

Discuss these questions with a partner.

1   Which social networking sites do you use? How long do you spend on them each week?
2   How has social networking changed the lives of young people today, compared to the previous generation of young people? Is it a change for the better?
3   Why do you need friends? Are online friends true friends?

Vocabulary preview

Number the expressions in the box to match the meaning of the underlined words in the sentences below.

___ different	___ develops	___ people you know	___ connections
___ evidence based on observation		___ ability to understand how someone feels	
___ someone who is interested only in him/herself			
___ help to develop	___ children who are changing into young adults		
___ always linked to people via technology			

1 Most of the people at the party were <u>acquaintances</u> rather than friends.
2 There is no <u>empirical evidence</u> that supports this idea.
3 The people I speak to online come from <u>diverse</u> backgrounds.
4 Technology <u>evolves</u> very quickly.
5 He's a <u>narcissist</u> who never asks about anyone else.
6 <u>Ties</u> between the two families have strengthened in recent years.
7 <u>Adolescents</u> are often unfairly criticized for bad behavior.
8 We need to <u>nurture</u> our young people so they become responsible adults.
9 We live in a <u>hyper-connected</u> society these days.
10 When I told him my bad news, he didn't show much <u>empathy</u>.

READING Are online "friends" a threat to development?

Before you read

Discuss these questions with a partner.

1 What are the advantages and disadvantages of young people using social networking sites?
2 Do you think the advantages outweigh the disadvantages? Why or why not?

Global reading

1 **You are going to read an excerpt from a child psychology book by Dr. Kristel Sharpe about the impact of social networking on a young person's emotional development. Can you guess what areas of impact she is going to mention?**

2 **Read _Are online "friends" a threat to development?_ on pages 10–11 to see if your ideas in exercise 1 are correct.**

IDENTIFYING THE WRITER'S POSITION

When a text contains different views, it is important to identify the writer's position compared to other people's positions.

To identify who the arguments belong to, look for names of people or groups of people. **_Turkle_** _also suggests that people are no longer comfortable being alone._

To identify if the writer agrees or disagrees with a viewpoint, look for:

• Positive or negative adjectives or adverbs, e.g., _not credible, interestingly_
• Opinion language such as _agree, disagree, true, untrue, believe, view_
• Linking phrases and signposts such as _however, therefore, although, in fact._

3 Which two statements describe the writer's position on social networking? What information in the text helped you identify the position?

1 Young people are losing their face-to-face friends.
2 There are advantages to having online friends.
3 People reveal too much information online.
4 Social networking is changing young people's personalities.

Critical thinking skill

WHAT EXACTLY IS AN ARGUMENT?

An argument is a statement of opinion supported by reasons or evidence. Without reasons or evidence, a statement is not an argument. Therefore, reasons and evidence must be identified within a text.

Friendships play an important role in our personal growth <u>because they help us to build trust</u>. (**statement** + <u>reason</u> = argument)

1 Read *Are online "friends" a threat to development?* again. Find and underline the points below in the text. The paragraph numbers are in parentheses.

1 The effect of new technology on our friendships is often discussed. (2)
2 Claims that social networking causes people to lose friendships are untrue. (3)
3 Young people can talk to a wider range of people online. (3)
4 Social networking can be advantageous for teenagers' emotional health. (4)
5 Social networking is causing young people to display different behavior. (5)
6 Through technology, people can fully control their friendships. (6)
7 Friendships in the real world are not easy to manage. (6)
8 People do not want to be on their own any more. (7)

2 Match points 1–8 to the evidence/reason a–f. One point matches more than once.

a A study by the Pew Internet and American Life Project ____
b A university study where people did not use social networks for a day ____
c Evidence from Larry D. Rosen ____
d No reason or evidence given ____
e Research by Sherry Turkle ____
f Research by Michigan State University ____

3 Which two points (1–8) in exercise 1 are not arguments? Why?

Developing critical thinking

Discuss these questions in a group.

1 Is social networking good for our emotional health? Is it changing our characters? Give reasons for your opinions.
2 What can young people, parents, schools, and the government do to reduce the problems of social networking?

ARE
ONLINE
"FRIENDS"
a threat to development?

An excerpt from *Nurturing a Child's Emotional Development* by psychologist Dr. Kristel Sharpe

[1] In chapter two, I discussed how vital childhood friendships are for a person's emotional development. They help us to build trust with people outside of the family and learn how to compromise, to share, and to manage conflict. When growing up, our friends provide the support we need to allow us to experiment with who we are. They give us feedback which helps to shape the behavior we adopt, and the people we ultimately become.

[2] The impact of technology on the nature of our friendships has been a much-debated topic since the meteoric rise of social networks. Advances in mobile technology and social networking websites mean we spend more time online than ever before. After all, if Facebook were a country, it would be the third largest in the world by population (*The Economist*, 2010). According to the Nielson Group (2010), it is not uncommon for people around the world to spend one in every four and a half minutes of their time sharing information online. It is therefore not surprising that so many psychologists, sociologists, and others are eager to give their thoughts on how this is impacting negatively on our society. It is only now, however, that we are starting to see the kind of empirical evidence necessary to differentiate fact from fiction.

[3] The biggest criticism leveled at social networking is that our young people are losing their offline friends to online friends who are unable to provide the same deep connection and emotional support and satisfaction. In fact there is a lot of research that shows these criticisms are generally unfounded.

Research by Allen et al. (2010) discovered that it is socially adjusted adolescents who are more likely to have a social networking profile than those who are not. One study carried out by the Pew Internet and American Life Project (2009) found that people are not substituting offline friends with online companions but are using them to support their offline relationships. They also found that social networks allow us to have discussions with a much more diverse set of people than in the real world, so we share knowledge with people from a wide variety of backgrounds.

[4] It is certainly true that our definition of friendship is evolving. An acquaintance we saw twice a year is now a friend we regularly talk to online. Yes, this relationship tie is weaker than one with a person in the real world, but there is evidence that young people still have a lot to gain from it. A study conducted by Michigan State University (2010) concluded that our virtual friendships provide social benefits and improve our psychological well-being. Our weaker ties contribute to this in particular. So, teenagers do not appear to be losing their face-to-face friends and the additional connections provided by social networking have proven to be beneficial.

[5] But there is one element of social networking that is deeply worrying and that is the fact that we find ourselves in a hyper-connected world: one where people access social media day and night, excited to make announcements about the tiniest details

of their lives. Research is starting to show that this culture is negatively affecting not our friendships but our character. Professor Larry D. Rosen, in his book *iDisorder*, presents evidence that social networking is turning us into narcissists. He says that young people who overuse social networking sites can become vain, aggressive, and display anti-social behavior in their offline lives. He says that sitting behind a screen makes them harsher and more mean-spirited. But perhaps an even more disturbing effect is that one of our most basic emotions seems to be disappearing—empathy. This is the emotion that bonds us together; it allows us to see the world from our friends' points of view. Without it, we are far less able to connect and form meaningful adult relationships. And yet a study has found that college students are actually 40% less empathetic than college students 30 years ago, with the largest decline occurring from the year 2000. In the 2010 study, fewer students described themselves as "soft-hearted" and more claimed that they are not affected when friends have bad fortune (O'Brien, 2010).

6 Sherry Turkle, a professor of social sciences at MIT, has made a fascinating observation about the impact of being plugged into your smartphone. Through her years of research, she has noticed that these devices permit us to have complete control over our friendships. Young people decide who they communicate with, when, and how. Friendships are unpredictable and difficult to deal with but social networks are allowing people to tidy them up and

manage them. If we do not want to be friends any more, a lengthy, awkward conversation is no longer needed. We simply click a button and unfriend them.

7 Turkle also suggests that people are no longer comfortable being alone. This is something confirmed by a study where 200 university students were asked to go without social media for 24 hours. Many admitted an addiction to their online social network; most complained that they felt cut off from family and friends. And yet being alone is a time, Turkle argues, when we self-reflect and get in touch with who we really are. It is only when we do this that we can make meaningful friendships with others. She believes, as is the title of her 2011 book, that we are simply "Alone Together."

8 These potential changes in our characters are rather disconcerting, so it is clear that we need to place our focus here when nurturing a child's development. Our young people may still have good offline relationships and may only use social networking for fostering face-to-face friendships. However, if they continue to develop the narcissistic tendencies outlined above, along with a reduction in empathy, a fear of the unpredictability of friendships, and an inability to self-reflect, our young people could well be in trouble. It is therefore here that I would like to move on to making suggestions about ways to encourage our young people to avoid the pitfalls of social networking so they can develop the kinds of friendships that are required to grow into well-adjusted and happy adults.

ACADEMIC KEYWORDS		
character	(n)	/ˈkerəktər/
conflict	(n)	/ˈkɑnˌflɪkt/
differentiate	(v)	/ˌdɪfəˈrenʃiˌeɪt/

Language development

SYNONYMS

Writers regularly use synonyms in their writing to avoid the repetition of words.

- Some synonyms mean exactly the same thing:

  *Some people choose to spend a lot of time with **relations**, whereas others prefer not to see **relatives** so frequently.*

- Some synonyms don't have exactly the same meaning:

  *For people who can no longer get out to see **friends**, pets can be very good **companions**.*

- Some synonyms have a different level of formality:

  *Some young people choose to **spend time** in virtual chat rooms. They often **hang out** at the mall as well.*

1 Match synonyms 1–10 with a–j. Find them in *Are online "friends" a threat to development?* To help you, use the paragraph number in parentheses.

1	manage (1)	___ a	provide (1)
2	allow (1)	___ b	discovered (3)
3	give (1)	___ c	adolescents (3)
4	eager (2)	___ d	tie (4)
5	impacting (2)	___ e	conducted (4)
6	connection (3)	___ f	excited (5)
7	carried out (3)	___ g	affecting (5)
8	found (3)	___ h	permit (6)
9	teenagers (4)	___ i	deal with (6)
10	nurturing (8)	___ j	fostering (8)

2 Rewrite the sentences using synonyms of the underlined words/expressions.

1 Few <u>teenagers</u> are <u>concerned</u> about the negative <u>effects</u> of our hyper-connected <u>world</u>.

2 It is not <u>unusual</u> for young people to form <u>online</u> <u>connections</u> with people they have never met in person.

3 Social networking <u>lets</u> us <u>make friendships</u> with more <u>varied</u> groups of people.

4 It is <u>untrue</u> that there has been a <u>decrease</u> in the number of <u>real life</u> friends people have.

5 Parts of our <u>personality</u> <u>seem</u> to be <u>changing</u> as a result of new technology.

6 Many people feel <u>isolated</u> when they cannot <u>contact</u> their friends.

3 Identify repeated words in the text below. Replace them with suitable synonyms.

The human brain is constantly changing, and neuroscientist Gary Small believes it is changing further because of new technologies. He believes that our ability to multitask is improving. He says that our ability to make decisions is improving. He also says that technology is improving our decision-making abilities. One study carried out with people aged between 55 and 76 using the Internet showed that the brains of the people who could already use the Internet showed much greater activity than those of the people who could not already use it.

SIMPLE AND PROGRESSIVE VERB FORMS

Simple verb forms tell us that an action or state occurs. They can include an action or state which is complete, habitual, or factual. Progressive verb forms emphasize duration or describe an incomplete, ongoing action.

Compare verb forms:

Present perfect simple	Connections provided by social networking **have proven** to be beneficial.
Present perfect progressive	Most young people **have been using** technology since they were small.
Past perfect simple	Young people who **had spent** a lot of time online found their exam results suffered.
Past perfect progressive	One young person admitted he **had been chatting** to friends online all night.
Future perfect simple	A new kind of social networking **will have become** popular before the end of the decade.
Future progressive	Young people all over the world **will be chatting** online to their friends this evening.

Verbs describing states are not used in the progressive form. These include verbs of perception, preferences, and mental states, e.g., *feel, hear, dislike, mind, believe, doubt.*

1 **Work with a partner. Discuss the pairs of example sentences in the box above. Why is a simple or progressive verb form used in each one?**

2 **Circle the best verb forms in this article.**

AMIR IS A SHY college student who has few friends and rarely speaks in class, but online he is outgoing, funny, and popular. In recent months, researchers around the world [1] **have carried out / have been carrying out** studies to find out whether social networking can help or hinder the social lives of people like Amir. So far, the research [2] **has shown / has been showing** that social networking and online learning environments are able to help shy people to form connections, especially those with low social skills. But it is not yet known whether social networking [3] **has helped / has been helping** them to connect better with the real world, or [4] **has taken / has been taking** them even further away from it.

It is not just social situations in which shy students like Amir can struggle; school can also be a problem. However, it seems that social networking sites may be able to help. The results of some Danish research showed that shy students [5] **had benefited / had been benefiting** from the use of a well-known social networking site during the study. The students [6] **had used / had been using** it in class to ask anonymous questions to the teacher, who [7] **had then replied / had then been replying** via computer. At the beginning of the study, shy students said they [8] **had lacked / had been lacking** in confidence in class for some time but at the end of the study they [9] **had begun / had been beginning** to feel more confident about their learning. As a result, researchers have said that they hope more schools and universities [10] **will have adopted / will be adopting** this technique by the end of the year.

3 **Work with a partner. Discuss why you chose each verb form in exercise 2.**

WRITING Writing an email

You are going to learn about different levels of formality in writing and how language changes. You are then going to rewrite an informal email so that it has the appropriate level of formality and tone for the reader, a college professor.

Writing skill

FORMALITY

When writing a text, it is important to think carefully about who will read it as this will determine the level of formality. We can show formality through the tone, the language used, punctuation, and the use of noun phrases (*There was a rapid increase in numbers.*) and verb phrases (*Numbers increased rapidly.*).

Formal/Academic	Neutral	Informal
Formal tone	Tone polite but friendly	Tone similar to speaking
Greater use of passive voice	Passive and active voice	Active voice
More noun phrases	More verb phrases	More verb phrases
No use of slang, idioms, phrasal verbs	Some use of phrasal verbs; no slang or idioms	Use of slang, idioms, phrasal verbs
No use of contractions or abbreviations	Use of contractions and some abbreviations	Use of contractions and abbreviations

1 **Read the texts and decide on the level of formality of each. What relationship do you think the writer has with the reader? Underline the features noted in the table above that give you this information.**

1 It is said that an increase in online communication will further have an impact on family life, both positively and negatively, although research has yet to show exactly what these effects will be.

2 I would be extremely grateful if you could supply further details of the nature of the problem you have with the product you purchased as soon as possible to allow a quick solution to be found.

3 So, as I was saying, it's gonna be great to finally meet up and talk through this project f2f. Hopefully we'll be able to get it up and running asap.

4 Would it be possible for us to get together at some stage during the week to discuss the research in greater detail? I know that you're very busy so I'd be happy to meet at a time convenient for you.

2 **Rewrite the email extracts below so that they are more appropriate for the reader listed in parentheses.**

1 (friend)
Would it be at all possible for you to contact me as soon as you can? I have a problem that I am unable to manage and require your assistance.

2 (your new college professor)
I'm really worried that I can't do my assignment in time and you'll fail it. Can I have an extension?

3 (a friend of a friend you have never met)
I'm Ahmed's friend. Can you help me with my research? Ahmed suggested it.

4 (a college professor you know well)
Here's my finished assignment. Enjoy it. Bye.

WRITING TASK

You are going to write an email to your college professor requesting a meeting to discuss an assignment you are having trouble with. You have been in the college professor's class for six months and have spoken to each other face-to-face several times.

Read an email between friends setting up a meeting. Underline the language that sets the informal tone of the message.

Audience:	a college professor
Context:	an email request for a meeting
Purpose:	apply an appropriate level of formality to a real-life task

Hi Joelle,

How are you? How was your weekend? Mine was hectic as usual!

Are you free later this week to get together and chat about the psychology project? I've been struggling with it and need a bit of help cos the deadline's fast approaching. I'm worried that if I don't get a move on, I'll end up rushing it. I really want to get a good grade for this one so need to put some work in.

How about tomorrow night? I've got an appointment in the afternoon but I'll be done by 6pm. Does 7pm sound okay? I can come to you if it's easier. I could even bring pizza if you like. Let me know asap.

Hopefully see you soon,

Allie

BRAINSTORM

How would you need to change the email above to make it appropriate for a college professor? Think about the following: tone, language, punctuation.

PLAN

Decide what information you should include in your email to your college professor. Decide how the email should be organized and the tone that you should use as this will determine the language and punctuation you use.

WRITE

Write your email in around 100 words. Make sure you use an appropriate tone. Check that you use any simple or continuous verb forms correctly and use synonyms where necessary to avoid repetition and create a cohesive text. Begin and end your email with appropriate expressions.

SHARE

Exchange your email with a partner. Read the checklist below and give feedback to your partner.

- Is the tone of the email appropriate to the reader?
- Does your partner begin and end the email appropriately?
- Does your partner use appropriate verb forms?
- Has your partner used synonyms where appropriate?

REWRITE AND EDIT

Consider your partner's comments and rewrite your email.

STUDY SKILLS Process writing and peer checking

Getting started

Discuss these questions with a partner.

1   When you write a text for your teacher, what do you usually do before you write? Why?
2   What procedure do you follow while you write? Why?
3   What do you do after you finish writing? Do you and your classmates ever check each other's work? Why or why not?

Scenario

Read the scenario and think about what Saif did right and what he could have done more effectively.

Saif was asked by his teacher to write an essay giving an analysis of the advantages and disadvantages of the Internet for communication. He read the question very carefully and did some research on the topic so that he could support his arguments with research. He wrote his essay in two hours and emailed it to his teacher with a friendly message.

Before handing in his essay, Saif's classmate Abdullah asked Saif to read his essay and give him feedback. Saif was happy to read it and told Abdullah that there were many mistakes and he needed more reasons to support his arguments.

When Saif received feedback on his essay from his teacher, he learned that his essay had a good balance of arguments with supporting points, but that it was not organized in a logical way and so it had been difficult to understand in many places. While he used good vocabulary, there were some spelling issues.

Consider it

Read the tips about process writing and peer checking. Which strategies do you already use? Which strategies do you think would be useful for you to try? Why?

1   **Brainstorm and select.** First, brainstorm ideas on the topic. Then, select those that you would like to include and discard the others. Research will help you to choose. Think about what you would like your text to achieve.
2   **Organize your writing.** A plan helps a piece of writing to be more structured and easy to read. Organize your ideas so they are in a logical order, for example using a mind map or a flowchart.
3   **Write the first draft.** Follow your plan so that your essay is well structured and you include all your points at the appropriate time.
4   **Revise your work.** Check that you have met your aim, that your ideas are organized effectively, and that you use a range of language with accuracy.
5   **Participate in peer checking.** A classmate who reads your writing will often notice things you have not. Asking a classmate to give you a summary of your text will also help you to know if you have achieved your aim.
6   **Give constructive feedback.** If a classmate asks you to give feedback on a piece of writing, start by telling him/her what you liked about it. Be positive wherever you can. When discussing parts of the writing that were unsuccessful, use softer language such as *Perhaps you could… / I'd suggest… / I think it'd be a good idea for you to…* It is much easier to accept criticism presented in this way.
7   **Write the second draft.** Address the problems that you and your classmate identified. With fresh eyes, read it through one final time.

Over to you

Discuss these questions with a partner.

1   Why do you think taking a process approach to writing can be effective?
2   What strategies do you use to help you to check your work? Why?
3   What experiences have you had with peer checking? What did you learn from them?

Games

READING	Identifying contrasts
CRITICAL THINKING	Identifying references to things outside the text
LANGUAGE DEVELOPMENT	Guessing meaning from context
	Expressing contrast
WRITING	Creating an outline

Discussion point

Discuss these questions with a partner.

1 Would you like your city or country to host an event like the Olympics® or the FIFA World Cup™? Why or why not?

2 How do cities benefit from hosting events like sports tournaments, trade fairs, or world expos? What are some of the drawbacks?

3 What city is going to host the next Olympics? What do you think this city needs to do to best prepare for it? Make a list.

Vocabulary preview

Write the bold words in the news article next to the definitions 1–8.

OAKTOWN to host cycling race

Mayor Jill Murphy announced today that Oaktown will be the site of next year's Mountain Challenge pro cycling event. "This event will create **revenue** from tourists and advertising," said Murphy, "so we expect to have a **surplus** after all the money is counted." In addition, the race gives the city a chance to make road repairs. "Our **return** on this investment will be more than **financial**, because better roads will benefit all of us for years to come," Murphy said.

The mayor also vowed to learn from the city's earlier problems hosting a marathon. The city could not stay within the **budget** it had planned for that event, and eventually had to go into **debt** to pay for it. Murphy joked that the cost of that event "exceeded the **gross domestic product** (GDP) of many small countries," adding, "This time it will be different, I promise."

1 _____ : an amount of money that is left over
2 _____ : the amount of money you plan to spend
3 _____ : involving money
4 _____ : an amount of money that you owe
5 _____ : the yearly value of goods and services in a country
6 _____ : a profit on money that you have invested
7 _____ : was greater than a number or amount
8 _____ : income from business activities or taxes

READING After the Games end: Risks and rewards of hosting the Olympics® 🇬🇧

Before you read

Discuss these questions with a partner.

1 Which cities have recently hosted the summer or winter Olympics? What did they do well? What problems were there?
2 What part of hosting the Olympic Games is probably the most expensive?

Global reading

IDENTIFYING CONTRASTS

Many academic texts develop the main idea by contrasting two events, people, places, or ideas. It is important to recognize these contrasts and identify the most significant ways in which the two things compared in the text are similar or different. Look for words or phrases that express contrast, such as *in contrast (to)*, *unlike*, *despite*, *in spite of*, and *nevertheless*.

1 **Read the report** *After the Games end: Risks and rewards of hosting the Olympics* **on pages 20–21, written by a consulting firm for a government committee on hosting the Olympics. According to the report, what is the most significant difference in how the Barcelona and Athens Olympics were planned?**

   a Barcelona did not need to construct any new sports venues.
   b The Barcelona organizers planned better to avoid long-term costs.
   c The Athens organizers did not connect the city to the seaside.
   d The security costs were much higher for the Athens Olympics.

2 Which city's organizers did these things? Complete the sentences with *Athens*, *Barcelona*, or *Both cities*.

1 _____ had a clear goal for hosting the Olympics.

2 _____ made a small profit from the Games.

3 _____ had debt after hosting the Olympics.

4 _____ had trouble getting the organizers to cooperate.

5 _____ saw certain costs rise due to unexpected events.

6 _____ improved the quality of life for residents and visitors.

Critical thinking skill

1 Read *After the Games end* again. Choose the three main arguments in the report. What evidence or reasons are given to support them?

___ 1 Cities need to set a clear goal for hosting the Olympics.

___ 2 Olympic host cities should let private businesses control the planning.

___ 3 It is crucial to prepare for the long-term impact of hosting the Olympics.

___ 4 A wide range of stakeholders need to be involved to ensure success.

___ 5 Increasing a city's prestige has no real financial value.

> **IDENTIFYING REFERENCES TO THINGS OUTSIDE THE TEXT**
>
> Many reports, papers, articles, and other texts refer to people, events, and facts that are not given or explained in the text. The author assumes that readers will know or understand these references. When a reference of this kind is not familiar, you can often use the context to infer a general idea of what the reference means.

2 Work in groups. What do these lines from the report refer to?

1 "To be fair, Greece was far from the only European nation accumulating debt at the time, as the region's subsequent years of financial difficulties showed."

2 "The chance to bring the Games back to their historic roots was another key motivation of the organisers."

3 "In addition, the events of September 2001 greatly increased the Games' security costs."

3 Read *After the Games end* again and answer these questions. Use references to things outside the text to help you.

1 Is the city in the report the best-known city in its country?

2 Will the construction of new sports venues be a good idea for this city?

3 Do the city's organizers have a history of cooperation?

4 What is the city's weather probably like?

Developing critical thinking

Discuss these questions in a group.

1 What potential benefits and risks of hosting the Olympics are mentioned in the report? Can you think of others? Which ones do you think are significant?

2 The report gives recommendations for cities planning an Olympic bid. Which is most important? What else would you recommend?

AFTER THE GAMES END:

Risks and rewards of hosting the Olympics® ⚡🇬🇧

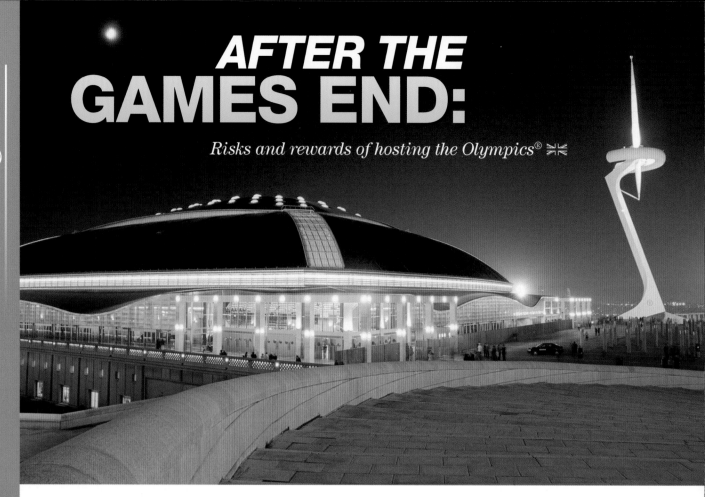

○ Introduction

[1] This report has been written to help the city's Olympic Committee prepare for their forthcoming bid for the summer Games. The factual information for this report is drawn from a variety of news reports in the *Independent*, *Guardian*, *Examiner*, *New York Times*, and *Forbes* magazine, as well as a study of the Barcelona Games, published in 2012, by Ferran Brunet i Cid of the *Universitat Autònoma de Barcelona*.

[2] In our report, we will first provide a general account and overview of the direct and indirect benefits that an Olympic host city can expect to receive, as well as the potential negative effects. We will then present a pair of case studies which illustrate the best and worst outcomes that can result. Finally, we will offer recommendations for committee members.

○ Benefits and risks

[3] The potential benefits and risks of hosting an Olympic Games can be broadly divided into three categories: financial considerations, the prestige that the Games can confer on a host city, and improvements to a city's quality of life.

[4] The financial impact of the Olympics is by far the most important consideration. The costs of hosting the Olympics can exceed tens of billions of dollars, and it is commonplace for budgets to double or even triple. In addition to the direct costs of hosting the Games (the opening and closing ceremonies, athletes'

village, security, etc.) cities often must build expensive new venues for lesser-known sports. However, an Olympic host city may also receive substantial revenue from ticket sales, tourist spending, corporate sponsorship, and television rights. (The host city receives half of the television revenue; an American network will pay US$4.38 billion to broadcast the four Olympics from 2014 to 2020.) Cities such as Los Angeles (1984) and Seoul (1988) actually made a large profit. In contrast, Montreal's massive debt from the 1976 Games took over 30 years to repay. Also, once constructed, sports venues incur additional maintenance costs long after the Games have ended, and these can be substantial, for example AUS$100 million per year after the 2000 Olympics in Sydney.

[5] While costs are the primary concern for a host city, there are other factors to consider. For one, hosting the Olympic Games confers prestige on a host city and country, which can lead to increased trade and tourism. The Olympics are also an opportunity to invest in projects that improve the city's quality of life, such as new transportation systems.

○ Case studies

[6] The following case studies represent what are generally thought to be an ideal outcome (Barcelona 1992) and a particularly negative outcome (Athens 2004) that resulted for the host cities.

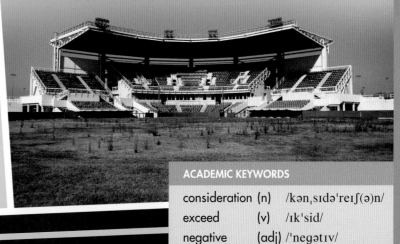
Barcelona 1992

[7] In contrast to other host cities who have often taken on the Games without clear objectives, the organisers of the Barcelona Olympics set one major goal: the transformation of Barcelona into one of Europe's great centres of tourism and business. For this reason, the organisers worked to minimise the direct costs of hosting the Games while focusing their investment on improvements that would benefit the city for years to come. The construction of sports venues accounted for less than 10% of the construction costs; the rest of the money went to expanding roads, green spaces, housing, hotels, and business centres. Most notably, the Olympic Village was built to reconnect the city with its waterfront. An attractive port was added, and over two miles of beaches were created. Much of this was the work of a well-coordinated partnership between government and business.

[8] In terms of its direct profit from the Games, Barcelona had a modest surplus of about $5 million. On the other hand, the positive effects in future years were immense. The improvements to the waterfront and roads greatly improved the quality of life. Furthermore, the Olympics helped transform Barcelona from an often-overlooked city to a prime destination for tourism and business. In 1990, it was ranked as only the 11th-best European city to do business in, but by 2011 it had soared to number four. Tourism doubled, and the Olympics generated over 20,000 permanent jobs for the city.

Athens 2004

[9] A crucial lesson to be learned from Athens 2004 is the importance of preparing for the long-term impact of hosting the Games. The Olympics left Athens and Greece billions of dollars in debt—the equivalent of €50,000 per family. (To be fair, Greece was far from the only European nation accumulating debt at the time, as the region's subsequent years of financial difficulties showed.)

[10] In addition, the sports venues that Athens built for the Games are mostly unused now, but have cost an estimated $775 million in maintenance since the Games ended. For economic reasons not all of this maintenance was kept up, and by 2012 as many as 21 of the 22 venues built for the 2004 Olympics stood abandoned.

[11] Despite these results, Athens began its planning on the right foot. Like Barcelona, it identified key strategic objectives for hosting the Games: attracting foreign investment, boosting exports, and increasing tourism. (The chance to bring the Games back to their historic roots was another key motivation of the organisers.) However, unlike Barcelona, the stakeholders in the Athens Games did not always cooperate well, with disagreements arising among businesses, government agencies, and political parties. Delays ensued, leading to cost increases. In addition, the events of September 2001 greatly increased the Games' security costs. In the end, the Olympics cost the equivalent of 5% of Greece's gross domestic product.

[12] Nevertheless, in many ways the 2004 Olympics improved the quality of life for the city. A modern, state-of-the art airport was built. Public transportation was expanded, resulting in a reduction in both traffic and pollution. Pleasant walkways were created to connect key sites in the city's historic centre and are enjoyed today by locals and tourists alike.

ACADEMIC KEYWORDS		
consideration	(n)	/kənˌsɪdəˈreɪʃ(ə)n/
exceed	(v)	/ɪkˈsiːd/
negative	(adj)	/ˈnegətɪv/

Recommendations

[13] In light of these outcomes, we recommend the following measures:

○ **Establish a clear goal.** Just as Barcelona did in 1992, our city can also use the Games to raise its profile to equal that of our better-known neighbours on the east coast.

○ **Carefully consider the future costs,** especially for maintaining venues for obscure and less popular sports such as indoor cycling, equestrianism, and fencing. In this city, where a single sport captures most people's attention, there may be little long-term return on the investment in these venues.

○ **Ensure cooperation among private and public stakeholders.** The city's recent experience with the expansion of the art museum will provide an excellent base for cooperation upon which to build.

○ **Expect the unexpected.** Events on the other side of the world can have a significant effect on budgets and schedules. Similarly, any city with weather like ours ought to plan for delays in events that are held outdoors.

[14] The Olympics present an excellent opportunity for the city to showcase its history, culture, and people. By following these recommendations, it is hoped that the city will reap the benefits of the Games for years to come.

Language development

GUESSING MEANING FROM CONTEXT

Authentic texts often contain so much unfamiliar vocabulary that it is not practical to look up every word in a dictionary. Instead, readers use the context to work out an approximate idea of a word's meaning. It is helpful to remember these points:

- A new word is often paired with a synonym or an antonym.

  A **modern, state-of-the-art** airport was built. (state-of-the-art = modern)

- A new word is often part of a collocation with familiar words, or frequently used together with familiar words.

  It is hoped that the city will **reap** the **benefits** of the Games for years to come. (reap benefits = get benefits)

- The meaning of a new word is often made clear by statistics or information given later in the sentence.

  Barcelona had a **modest** surplus of about $5 million. (modest = relatively small)

- Some new words mean the same as similar-looking words.

  It is **commonplace** for budgets to double. (commonplace = common)

1 **Complete these lines from *After the Games end*. The words in bold are synonyms of, or part of collocations with the words in the box.**

benefits	costs	exports	less popular	overview	prestige

1 … a general **account** and _____ of the direct and indirect benefits … (para. 2)

2 The potential _____ and **risks** of hosting an Olympic Games … (para. 3)

3 … sports venues **incur** additional maintenance _____ long after the Games … (para. 4)

4 Hosting the Olympic Games **confers** _____ on a host city … (para. 5)

5 … attracting foreign investment, **boosting** _____, and increasing tourism. (para. 11)

6 … maintaining venues for **obscure** and _____ sports … (para. 13)

2 **Match these words from *After the Games end* with the information.**

1 … **substantial** revenue … (para. 4)   ___ a from 11th to 4th
2 … **massive** debt … (para. 4)   ___ b $4.38 billion in television rights
3 … by 2011 it had **soared** … (para. 8)   ___ c businesses, government agencies, and political parties
4 … **stakeholders** … did not always   ___ d 30 years to repay
  cooperate well (para. 11)

3 **In groups, work out the meaning of the bold words in exercises 1 and 2.**

4 **Find these words in *After the Games end* and try to work out the meanings. Compare answers with a partner.**

outcomes (para. 2)	partnership (para. 7)	showcase (para. 14)

EXPRESSING CONTRAST

There are a number of ways to show how two ideas, things, or people are different.

- Use *although*, *(even) though*, *while*, and *whereas* before a clause (subject + verb).

  While costs are the primary concern for a host city, there are other factors to consider.

- Use *in contrast*, *however*, *nevertheless*, *nonetheless*, and *on the other hand* at the beginning of a sentence or after a semicolon. A comma is necessary after each of these words or phrases.

  In contrast, Montreal's massive debt took over 30 years to repay.

- You can use phrases such as *in contrast to*, *despite*, *in spite of*, and *unlike* followed by a noun and a comma.

  In contrast to other host cities, the organisers of the Barcelona Olympics set one goal.

- You can also use *however*, *though*, *nevertheless*, and *nonetheless* after a comma at the end of a sentence.

  Hosting the Olympics raises national pride. It comes at a cost, **though**.

---

1 **Circle the correct word or phrase to complete the paragraphs.**

   ¹**In contrast / In contrast to** the Olympics®, the FIFA World Cup™ has been held all over the world, including in Africa and South America. Rio de Janeiro, Brazil, was chosen to host the 2016 Olympics; ² **however, / despite**, and it is likely that future Olympic Games will be held in Africa.

   The 1996 Atlanta Games made a profit. ³ **Though, / However,** many felt that the use of advertisements at those Games was excessive. These advertisements were very good business for the sponsors, ⁴ **though / in contrast**.

   Montreal lost an enormous amount of money on the 1976 Olympics. ⁵ **In contrast, / In contrast to,** the 1984 L.A. Olympics made a large profit. ⁶ **While / Despite** a rough start, the '84 Games were a great success. Why did L.A. succeed where others had failed? ⁷ **Whereas / Unlike** the Olympics before it, the L.A. Games were run mostly by private businesses.

2 **Complete the sentences with your own ideas. Compare answers in groups.**

   1 **Even though** hosting the Olympics is expensive, I believe …
   2 American football is very popular in the U.S. **In contrast**, most people in my country …
   3 **Unlike** events like swimming and sprinting, the marathon …
   4 Sports like cycling and equestrian require expensive equipment; **on the other hand**, …
   5 **Despite** the popularity of football, many people …

Language development

WRITING A compare and contrast report

You are going to learn about creating an outline that will make your writing clearer and better organized. You are then going to use this skill to write a report that compares the effect of a major sporting event on two different host cities or countries.

Writing skill

CREATING AN OUTLINE

An outline is a document that helps you plan an essay before you start writing. It will help you better understand your ideas and will make your essay more organized.

- Begin with an **introduction**. This paragraph should state the essay's main idea.
- Think of **arguments** that explain, support, or develop your idea. Make each argument a separate section in your outline.
- For each argument, think of **details**, **examples**, and **reasons** that support the argument. Write these points underneath the arguments they support.
- **Organize** your points. Finish one argument or idea before beginning the next one.
- End with a **conclusion** that restates your main idea and arguments.

Add the information in the box to the outline of an essay comparing the effects of the 1994 and 2010 FIFA World Cup™ on the host nations.

a	Fans already knew the U.S. well; little changed
b	90% of fans said they would visit South Africa again
c	Football already popular; attendance didn't rise
d	Event went smoothly, no major problems
e	In 1994, over 80,000 attended U.S.-Brazil match
f	World Cup had significant but different effects on each nation

I INTRODUCTION

1. Background of World Cup—has earned billions and transformed nations; 1994 World Cup in U.S.; 2010 World Cup in South Africa

2. Main Idea: 1994 World Cup made football popular in the U.S., while 2010 World Cup brought prestige to South Africa

II WORLD CUP'S IMPACT ON POPULARITY OF FOOTBALL

1. South Africa: _____

2. United States: Football became more popular and successful

   - In 1989, only 3,000 fans attended U.S. team matches

   - _____

   - Today, more youth football teams than baseball teams in U.S.

III WORLD CUP'S IMPACT ON PRESTIGE OF HOST COUNTRY

1. United States: _____

2. South Africa: Fans' impressions greatly improved

   - Before the Cup: Media worried about crime and delays

   - During the Cup: _____

   - After the Cup: _____

   - After the Cup: TripAdvisor (world's biggest travel site) ranks Cape Town as the world's top travel destination

IV CONCLUSION

_____

_____

_____

_____

WRITING TASK

Imagine your country has asked you to recommend whether it should host the World Cup or another major event such as the Olympics or a world expo. You are going to write a report comparing the effect that this event has had on two previous host countries. Recommend whether your country should host the event.

Audience:	government officials
Context:	a government report or white paper
Purpose:	compare and contrast, then give recommendations

Look at the outline on page 24 again. Which part of the writing task does the outline cover? Which part would you need to add to the outline?

a Compare the effect of an event on two host cities or countries

b Recommend whether your city should host the event

BRAINSTORM
Make a list of things your country would need to do in order to host the event. Are there enough stadiums, airports, hotels, trains, and so on?

PLAN
Decide whether your country should host the event and why. Think about the following:
- How would your country benefit from the event in the short term?
- What long-term effects would it have on the country?
- How would the country's economy, reputation, culture, and quality of life change?

Create an outline for your essay. Use the outline structure on page 24 as a guide. (If you prefer, you can use the outline to write an essay about South Africa and the U.S.) Add a section that recommends whether your country should host the event, and why.

WRITE
Write your essay in around 300 words. Use your outline as you write to make your ideas clear and organized. Include expressions of contrast and the new vocabulary terms you have learned in this unit.

SHARE
Exchange essays with a partner. As you read your partner's essay, think about the following points:
- Does the essay compare and contrast two host cities or countries?
- Does the essay include the writer's recommendations?
- Compare the essay and the writer's outline. Did the writer follow the outline?
- Did the writer correctly use expressions of contrast and new vocabulary?
- Do you have any suggestions to improve the essay?

REWRITE AND EDIT
Consider your partner's comments and rewrite your essay.

STUDY SKILLS Finding an idea to write about

Getting started

Discuss these questions with a partner.

1   When you write an essay for school, how do you decide what to write about?
2   When do you usually think of the point you want to make about the essay topic: before you begin to write, while you're writing, or after you've finished the first draft of your essay?

Scenario

Read the scenario and think of at least one thing Hassan could have done to improve the idea in his essay.

Consider it

Look at the tips for finding an idea to write about. Which ones did Hassan keep in mind? Which ones could have helped Hassan?

1   Decide on an idea for your essay before you write.
2   Before you begin, you should be able to describe your idea in one or two clear sentences.

  It is often said that the Olympic Games bring different nations closer together, but the way the Games are shown on television actually makes nations more isolated from one another.

3   An idea is different from a topic; it is also different from the arguments that support the idea.
  Topic: How the Olympic Games are shown on television.
  Arguments:

  · Each nation broadcasts only the sports that they are good at or enjoy.

  · The news media focus only on which countries have won the most medals, which encourages pointless competition among nations.

4   A good idea comes from your own thinking and reflection, and doesn't simply repeat information you've read in another place.

Over to you

Discuss these questions with a partner.

1   Which of the tips above do you already use?
2   Which of the tips do you think are most important?
3   What are some things you can do to think of an idea to write about?
4   How will you use the advice above to help you in your next writing assignment?

Hassan is a first-year engineering major who is taking a required course in composition. He was recently asked to write an essay on the question, "What do the Olympic Games mean to you?" Because this was not a question Hassan had thought about before, he spent a few days reading about the most recent Games and reflecting.

Hassan prefers to plan, so he did not begin writing until he had a good idea of what he wanted to write about. Finally, he had an idea: how the Olympics are shown on television. This seemed very interesting, and he knew he could write a few pages about it, so he began the essay as soon as he thought of the idea.

He was sure he would complete the essay quickly, but after a few hours, Hassan realized that he wasn't actually sure of what he wanted to say.

In the end, it took a few days to finish the essay, and his professor said it had an interesting topic but didn't have a clear idea. It was a frustrating experience that Hassan would not like to repeat.

Nostalgia

READING	Understanding analogies in a text
CRITICAL THINKING	Identifying sources of information
LANGUAGE DEVELOPMENT	Reporting information
	Condensing information with compound adjectives
WRITING	Transition sentences

Discussion point

Discuss these questions with a partner.

1 What stage of life do you think most people remember as the happiest?
  What stage do most people remember as the most difficult?

2 What types of things do we store in our memories?

3 Look at the situations below. What types of things do you need to remember
  in order to do well in each situation?

getting along with family   making new friends   playing a game or sport
preparing a meal   taking an exam   traveling from home to work/school

Vocabulary preview

1 Complete the quiz with the words in the box.

> eyewitnesses   hippocampus   long-term   neuroscientists
> perceptions   recall   short-term   stable

HOW MUCH DO YOU KNOW ABOUT MEMORY?

Decide if these statements about memory are true or false.

1 About 40% of people can _____ being newborn babies.
2 The more often _____ describe what they saw, the less _____ their memories become.
3 All memories are stored in a tiny part of the brain called the _____.
4 Almost all of our _____—what we see, hear, taste, smell, and feel— are immediately forgotten.
5 Your _____ memory can remember only about seven things for 30 seconds.
6 Once something enters your _____ memory, you will never forget it.
7 After decades of studying the brain, _____ have developed drugs that can give laboratory mice perfect memories.

2 Which statements in the quiz do you think are true? Which are false?

READING The shifting sands of memory

Before you read

Work with a partner. Discuss the questions below.

1 What is your earliest memory? Is it strong or faint?
2 What are some of the strongest memories you have from your childhood?
3 What are some things that people often have trouble remembering or aren't able to recall?

Global reading

1 Read *The shifting sands of memory,* on pages 30–31, written by a journalist for a popular science magazine. Which statement best describes the writer's position?

a Neuroscience has shown that memory is stable and accurate.
b It is acceptable for advertisers to manipulate people's memories.
c Memory affects nearly every area of life, yet it is surprisingly unreliable.
d It is wrong for scientists to plant false memories in people.

UNDERSTANDING ANALOGIES IN A TEXT

An analogy is a figure of speech that shows how one thing is similar to another. Analogies often use the structure *X is like Y*, for example: **A unicycle is like a bicycle**, *except it has only one wheel.*

In academic writing, analogies are often used to make an idea clearer by showing how an unfamiliar concept is similar to something that readers know well. Because writers will often use analogies to develop and expand their main idea over the course of a text, it is important to recognize and follow them.

---

2 Read the *The shifting sands of memory* again. Check the analogies that the writer mentions in the text.

1 ☐ Memory is like a video recorder.

2 ☐ Memory is like an elderly grandmother.

3 ☐ Memory is like a computer's hard drive.

4 ☐ Memory is like a recipe.

5 ☐ Memory is like a seahorse.

6 ☐ Memory is like a pill.

3 Explain the analogies you checked in your own words.

4 Which of the analogies in exercise 2 does the writer think is best? Why?

5 Look at the statements from the quiz in *Vocabulary preview*. According to *The shifting sands of memory*, which are true? Which are false?

Critical thinking skill

IDENTIFYING SOURCES OF INFORMATION

In academic essays, news reports, opinion pieces, and similar texts, writers present information from a variety of sources in order to inform or persuade readers. For this reason, it is important to identify the sources of these facts and claims as you read. Think about where the writer gets this information and whether the source is credible. As a general rule, good writers will identify their sources of information as clearly as possible and only use reliable sources.

1 Read *The shifting sands of memory* again and find the source for each piece of information. (Sometimes no source is given.)

1 There were no lambs on the writer's grandparents' farm. (para. 2)

2 We tend to remember the past as better than it really was. (para. 3)

3 We rely on our memories to do well in school. (para. 5)

4 Eyewitness recollections become less accurate with each retelling. (para. 5)

5 You can remember only about seven items for 30 seconds in your short-term memory. (para. 7)

6 A drug called anisomycin erased memories in laboratory rats. (para. 10)

7 Advertising can cause people to have false memories. (para. 12)

2 Work with a partner. Find three more pieces of information from *The shifting sands of memory* and their sources (if any).

3 Discuss the information and sources in exercises 1 and 2.

1 Which information do you think is most credible? Why? Which is less credible? Why?

2 Which of the sources used in the magazine article would you not expect to find in:

   a a news report   **b** an academic essay on this subject

Developing critical thinking

Discuss these questions in a group.

1 Do you agree with Elizabeth Loftus that our memories are unreliable? What are the strongest and weakest reasons that support this position?

2 Would you ever want to use the "memory pill" described in the article? Make a list of advantages and disadvantages of this drug.

3 Imagine that humans had perfect memories and never forgot anything. Would the world be a better place? Make a list of advantages and disadvantages.

The SHIFTING SANDS of Memory

¹ For most of us, it is not difficult to conjure up rosy memories of our childhoods. Perhaps you recall a favorite pet, a much-loved toy, or a special place. For this writer, that place was my grandparents' old farm, where I played with flocks of friendly lambs and feasted on warm, delicious chocolate chip cookies straight from my nana's oven.

² However, it's a funny thing about that memory—it turns out that most of it isn't true. According to my mother, I was actually miserable during my visits to the farm. She says that there were no lambs—I had that mixed up with a visit to a petting zoo when I was older—but rather a herd of surly cows that frightened me to the point of tears. As for my grandmother's cookies, I recently persuaded her to bake them for me again, and the results were dry and disappointing.

³ Perhaps my nana's baking skills have deserted her, but that still doesn't explain the other inaccuracies in my recollections. The reality is that our memories are simply not that reliable. According to Elizabeth Loftus, a professor of psychology at the University of California and an authority on memory, "Our memories have a superiority complex. We remember we got better grades than we did, that we gave more money to charity than we did, that our kids walked and talked earlier than they really did."

⁴ In fact, Loftus and her colleagues have learned that our memories do not just exaggerate; in some cases, they out-and-out lie. In one well-known experiment, Loftus asked test subjects to read aloud four descriptions of events which, they were told, were gathered from family members and had actually happened to them. In fact, only three were true, while the fourth—an account of being lost in a shopping mall at age five—had never happened to any of the subjects. In follow-up interviews, however, 25% of the subjects claimed that they clearly remembered the false incident, often embellishing the "memory" with vivid details straight from their own imaginations.

⁵ The implications of these findings are far-ranging. We all know that childhood memories have profound and long-lasting effects on our relationships with our family, friends, and spouses. If we can't trust our memories, how can we trust the people closest to us? Memories also play a crucial role in self-esteem; we are what we remember. We depend on our memories to do well at school, to remember vital skills in the workplace, to keep us safe by reminding us of past mistakes, and to cheer us up by recalling past triumphs. In addition, the police rely on accurate eyewitness accounts to bring criminals to justice and keep the public safe, but Marc Green, an expert on memory and witness testimony, has stated that these recollections become less accurate with each retelling.

⁶ What is memory, anyway, and why does it play tricks on us? We often imagine that memory is like a video recorder that captures every detail with perfect accuracy; the memories are then stored complete and intact like files on a hard drive. However, recent research suggests that a better analogy for memory might actually be my grandmother's cookie recipe. Like the ingredients in a recipe, a single memory is actually a collection of separate pieces stored in different places all over the brain—a sound here, a smell there, a flash of color over there—and each time we remember an event, we are actually reassembling the memory in our heads. A lot can go wrong when you bake a batch of cookies, and similarly, many scientists are now concluding that the very act of remembering can sometimes distort the memory itself.

7 There is still much to learn about how memories are formed in the brain, but the basic ideas are clear. All memories begin as perceptions—what we see, hear, taste, smell, and feel. Most perceptions are immediately forgotten, but a few enter our short-term memory. Studies show that short-term memory is very limited; you can remember only about seven items for no longer than 30 seconds.

8 At this point, researchers believe that a tiny seahorse-shaped structure in the brain called the hippocampus plays a crucial role in deciding which events are worth saving as long-term memories. (Interestingly, it takes a year or more for a newborn baby's hippocampus to fully develop, which is why you don't have any memories from your first year of life.) If the hippocampus retains an event, it takes the perceptions from your short-term memory and stores them in different parts of the brain. Each time you remember the event, an electrical impulse reconnects these separate perceptions, creating a memory. In other words, the memory is recreated each time you recall it.

9 This is where things can go wrong. We can forget a step in the recipe, or we can mistakenly add the wrong ingredients. Perceptions from other events can get mixed up in the original memory, as was the case with the petting zoo I added to my memory of my grandparents' farm. Or, as the Loftus experiments indicate, information and ideas from outside sources can get mixed into the dough.

10 Despite the findings of Loftus and other psychologists, neuroscientists had always assumed that the more often you remember an event, the more stable the memory. These assumptions are now being challenged by young researchers such as Karim Nader at McGill University in Canada. Nader demonstrated that a drug called anisomycin can actually erase memories in laboratory rats. Rats are not people, of course, but Nader argues that the same principles apply to human memory. In fact, a later experiment with human subjects found that a drug called propranolol reduced the intensity of traumatic memories of war and violence.

11 The practical implications of this research are obvious. Long-suffering people with tragic memories could be released from the agonies of the past. As for the rest of us, wouldn't it be wonderful to come home after a bad day at the office, pop a "memory pill," and forget all about it?

12 In addition to this, Loftus and other psychologists believe that we can exploit the flexibility of human memory to achieve a number of aims, some more admirable than others. In one study, called "Healthier Eating Could Be Just a False Memory Away," Loftus and her colleagues explain how they convinced subjects that they loved to eat asparagus as children, which led to a "greater desire to eat asparagus." (A similar study convinced its subjects that strawberry ice cream used to make them sick.) If a little deception helps us eat better, do the ends justify the means? And what about other studies that show how advertising can trick us into falsely remembering happy experiences at fast food restaurants and amusement parks?

13 No matter where the science leads us, one fact remains the same. Memories are the foundations of our lives. They are the glue that holds together families, friendships, and marriages. Good or bad, accurate or not, where would we be without them? Perhaps what really matters isn't how my nana's cookies actually tasted all those years ago, but the happy times we spent together baking and enjoying them.

HOW ARE MEMORIES FORMED?

1 Perceptions enter the brain—most are immediately forgotten.

↓

2 Short-term memory stores a few things for about 30 seconds.

↓

3 The hippocampus chooses some things for long-term memory.

↓

4 Different perceptions are stored in different parts of the brain.

↓

5 The memory is recreated each time you recall it.

ACADEMIC KEYWORDS

aim	(n)	/eɪm/
assume	(v)	/əˈsum/
crucial	(adj)	/ˈkruʃ(ə)l/

Language development

REPORTING INFORMATION

Writers use reporting verbs such as *say*, *state*, and *explain* to give sources of information. These verbs are usually followed by *that* and a noun clause.

*My mother **says** that there were no lambs on the farm.*
(The source of the information is the writer's mother.)

Many reporting verbs are neutral in meaning, but others express the writer's attitude to the information. Verbs such as *show*, *prove*, and *demonstrate* mean that the writer believes that the information is true, or a proven fact.

*Nader **demonstrated** that a drug can erase memories in rats.*
(The writer believes Nader proved that the drug erased memories in rats.)

Other reporting verbs such as *claim*, *suggest*, and *argue* mean that the writer does not believe that the information has been proven.

*Rats are not people, but Nader **argues** that the same principles apply to human memory.*
(The writer believes Nader has not yet proven that the same principles apply.)

You can use *according to* to show sources of information and *in fact* to report information that you believe is true.

***According to** the subjects in the experiment, these events really happened, but **in fact** they were fictional episodes.*

Note: verbs such as *believe* and *learn* are used for people but not for studies or reports.

1 **The reporting verbs in the box are used in *The shifting sands of memory*. Find them in the text and discuss their meanings. Then complete the chart.**

| ~~argue~~ | assume | believe | claim | conclude | ~~demonstrate~~ |
| explain | find | indicate | learn | ~~say~~ | show | state | suggest |

Neutral meaning	The author thinks the information...	
	... has been proven	... has **not** been proven
say	*demonstrate*	*argue*

2 **Circle the correct reporting verb to complete the sentences.**

1 The report **shows / claims** that memory is reliable, but offers no evidence.

2 A convincing new study has **assumed / found** that doing crossword puzzles improves people's memory.

3 The effect of caffeine on memory is still unclear; some studies have **argued / demonstrated** that it has a positive effect, while others have **shown / suggested** this isn't true.

4 A recent experiment in Indonesia **concluded / believed** that elderly people who eat a great deal of tofu have a higher risk of memory loss.

5 The data from the experiment **learn / show** that a diet high in fish is good for people's memory.

6 A 2007 study in Canada clearly **shows / argues** that people with long-term back or neck pain often have trouble remembering things.

3 Rewrite the sentences in exercise 2 with the reporting expressions in parentheses.

1 (according to) _According to the report, memory is reliable._

2 (in fact) _____

3 (according to … according to) _____

_____

4 (according to) _____

5 (in fact) _____

6 (in fact) _____

CONDENSING INFORMATION WITH COMPOUND ADJECTIVES

A compound adjective is an adjective composed of two words, such as *well-known*, *ice-cold*, and *fast-paced*. Writers use compound adjectives with past and present participles to present information in a shorter way.

… effects that last a long time → **long-lasting** effects

… a toy that you loved very much → a **much-loved** toy

Form	Example
Compound adjectives with a present participle usually describe what something does.	a fast-moving train an English-speaking tour guide
Compound adjectives with a past participle usually describe an action that a person or thing receives.	a well-known actress a home-made cake
Compound adjectives with a noun + -ed usually describe what something looks like or has.	a blond-haired woman a blue-eyed man

1 Circle the correct compound adjective to complete the sentences.

1 Even though he is a **well-paid** / **well-paying** lawyer, Ahmed lives in a tiny house and doesn't own a car.

2 The film is a **heartbroken** / **heartbreaking** story of a **hard-worked** / **hard-working** man who loses everything.

3 How could you forget Jill? She was the **pink-haired** / **pinked-hair** woman in the **brightly colored** / **brightly coloring** dress.

4 A **smooth-talked** / **smooth-talking** salesman sold Joseph a memory training course that didn't work at all.

5 I'll never forget our team's **record-broken** / **record-breaking** performance in this year's championships.

6 In **densely populated** / **densely populating** cities, taxi drivers need to memorize a large number of street names and transportation routes.

2 Rewrite the sentences. Replace the bold words with a compound adjective.

1 Jane is a person **who has a strong will** and rarely changes her mind.

2 Painful memories are often the cause of problems **that have deep roots**.

3 It's easy to remember Todd Splodd because of his name **that sounds odd**.

4 Because Jim is a person **who has an open mind**, he is always learning new things.

5 This is a documentary **that never ends!** When will it be over?

6 To remember the prefix *tri-*, think of a triangle or a tricycle, which is a bicycle **that has three wheels**.

WRITING Analyzing a memory

You are going to learn about writing transition sentences to connect one paragraph to the next. You are then going to use this skill to write an essay that analyzes how accurate a personal memory is.

Writing skill

TRANSITION SENTENCES

Effective transition sentences are important elements in well-written academic essays. A transition sentence appears at the beginning of a paragraph. It shows how the ideas in the previous paragraph are connected to those in the new one. Techniques for writing effective transition sentences include:

- Use *this, these, that,* and *those* to show a link to the previous paragraph.

  The implications of **these** findings are far-ranging.

- Use words such as *however, although, despite,* and *like* to show how ideas are connected.

  Despite the findings of Loftus and other psychologists, neuroscientists had always assumed ...

- Use fixed expressions such as *on the other hand, next,* and *in addition* to signal a different point of view, a new step in a process, a related idea, and so on.

  At this point, researchers believe that a tiny seahorse-shaped structure in the brain called the hippocampus plays a crucial role ...

Read the student report about a study on memory and the transition sentences in the box. Choose the best transitions to complete the text.

a	There are two important details that should be discussed.
b	This difference in wording is significant for two reasons.
c	The implications of these findings are far-ranging.
d	As a result of this, the two questions yielded very different responses.
e	Different groups of subjects responded very differently.

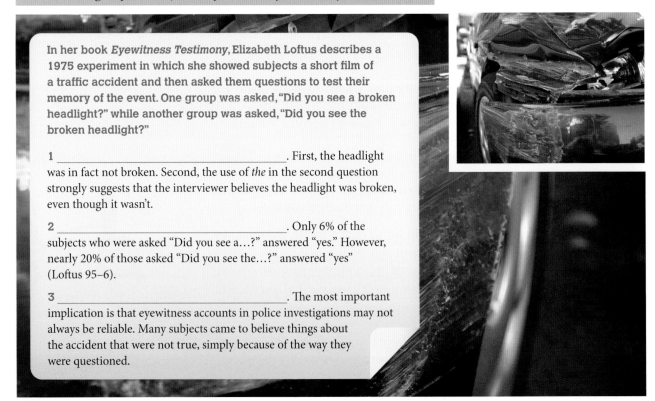

In her book *Eyewitness Testimony*, Elizabeth Loftus describes a 1975 experiment in which she showed subjects a short film of a traffic accident and then asked them questions to test their memory of the event. One group was asked, "Did you see a broken headlight?" while another group was asked, "Did you see the broken headlight?"

1 _____. First, the headlight was in fact not broken. Second, the use of *the* in the second question strongly suggests that the interviewer believes the headlight was broken, even though it wasn't.

2 _____. Only 6% of the subjects who were asked "Did you see a...?" answered "yes." However, nearly 20% of those asked "Did you see the...?" answered "yes" (Loftus 95–6).

3 _____. The most important implication is that eyewitness accounts in police investigations may not always be reliable. Many subjects came to believe things about the accident that were not true, simply because of the way they were questioned.

WRITING TASK

How accurate are memories? Write a short essay on this question, using examples from your own life, supported by evidence from the texts on pages 30–31 and 34. Use transition sentences and include reporting verbs and compound adjectives to condense information where possible.

Read the model text. Underline the transition sentences. Circle the reporting verbs or expressions and the compound adjectives.

Audience: a university professor
Context: formative assessment in the form of an essay
Purpose: use evidence to support ideas

Writing skills

Although memories are generally reliable, research and personal experience both suggest that childhood memories are often less accurate. According to one well-known study by memory expert Elizabeth Loftus, up to 25% of subjects can have vivid, but false, memories of events that never happened to them.

These findings are reflected in some of my own recollections. In one of my earliest memories, my mother fell asleep while we were coming home from school on a city bus. I remember being truly frightened. Would we miss our stop? Luckily, she woke up in time.

According to my mother, this memory is false. She says there were no bus routes near my school, and she found a long-forgotten bus map that demonstrated this fact. She also claims that she may have appeared to be asleep on another bus trip, but was only "resting her eyes."

These inaccuracies show how early memories can be distorted. Some details are likely to be true, while others are simply false, and perceptions from different times and events may have combined to form a single memory.

BRAINSTORM

1 Quickly re-read the texts on pages 30–31 and 34. Make a list of evidence that you find interesting.
2 Make a list of things that you know happened to you as a child. How clearly or accurately do you remember each event?

PLAN

Decide on an answer to the question, "How accurate are memories?" Then choose evidence from the texts and a childhood memory that support your view.

Create an outline for your essay.

- Begin by answering the question, "How accurate are memories?" in one or two simple sentences.
- Give evidence from the texts that supports your view.
- Briefly describe a childhood memory and explain how it is or isn't accurate.
- Explain how the childhood memory supports your answer to the question, "How accurate are memories?"

WRITE

Write your essay in around 300 words. Make sure to use transition sentences to make clear connections between the ideas in each paragraph. Use reporting verbs to give information and compound adjectives to condense information.

SHARE

Exchange essays with a partner. As you read your partner's essay, think about the following points:

- Does the essay give a clear answer to the question, "How accurate are memories?"
- Did the writer use evidence from the texts and a childhood memory to support this view?
- Did the writer effectively use transition sentences, reporting verbs, and compound adjectives?

REWRITE AND EDIT

Consider your partner's comments and rewrite your essay.

Eyewitness testimony

by Stella Cottrell

Eyewitness testimony

Eyewitness testimony may be useful in a number of circumstances, such as:

- people who saw or experienced accidents, crime and disasters first-hand;
- people who lived through historic events including the more distant past;
- clients' accounts of experiences and/or services received;
- patients' accounts of their experiences.

Levels of accuracy

Untruth

Personal testimonies can provide invaluable evidence, but they are not always accurate.

Interviewees may not reveal the true case because they:

- may want to be helpful, so say what they think the interviewer wants to hear;
- may not like the interviewer;
- may be trying to protect somebody;
- may not remember anything, but like the attention of being interviewed;
- may have a vested interest in the outcome, so benefit from concealing the truth;
- may be being bullied or intimidated and be scared of speaking out;
- may have promised to keep a secret.

If using interviews to gather evidence, remember that the interviewee may have complex motivations for presenting the picture that they give.

Lack of expertise and insider knowledge

The witness may lack information such as expert knowledge or details of why something was taking place which would enable them to make sense of what they saw. They may have seen a camera crew filming a fight in the street as they passed by one afternoon. However, they would not necessarily know whether they were watching a real fight at which a camera crew happened to attend, or whether the fight was staged deliberately for a TV drama. It may also be the case that the interviewee misunderstood what was asked of them.

The limits of memory

Loftus, in *Eyewitness Testimony* (1979), demonstrated, for legal use, how unreliable the memory can be. In one experiment, participants were shown a film of an accident and some were then asked how fast a white car was travelling when it passed a barn. A week later, 17% of those who had been asked this question reported that they had seen a barn in the film, even though there had been no barn. This compared with only 3% of the other viewers. Common memory mistakes include the following.

- Errors in perception: making mistakes about what you have seen and heard.
- Errors in interpretation: misinterpreting what you have seen.
- Errors of retention: simply forgetting.
- Errors of recall: remembering the event inaccurately. Our memory may be altered by going over the event in our mind, discussing it, hearing other people's accounts, or hearing about similar events.
- Composite memories: our brain can blend aspects from several events into one, without us being aware this is happening.

Corroborating sources

It is usually necessary to find other sources of information that corroborate a witness testimony. This can include other witnesses but may also be, for example:

- official records from the time;
- other witness testimony;
- TV footage of the events;
- newspaper, police, social work or court records;
- photographs taken at the time;
- information about similar events that happened elsewhere but which might throw light on the event being considered.

Risk

READING	Summarizing
CRITICAL THINKING	Assessing whether research supports an argument
LANGUAGE DEVELOPMENT	Adjective + preposition collocations
	Infinitive phrases
WRITING	Avoiding plagiarism

Discussion point

Discuss these questions with a partner.

1 What risks do people take in these areas of their lives?

> family   money   social life and friendships
> sports and leisure   travel   work

2 What is the biggest risk you have taken in your life so far? How did you feel about it?

3 What risks do you think you may have to take in the future? How do you feel about that?

Vocabulary preview

Complete the paragraph with the words in the box.

> biological makeup   consequences   disregard   peer pressure
> personality trait   seek   sound judgment   susceptibility

Why do some people actively (1) _____ risky activities and participate in them
with complete disinhibition or (2) _____ for the (3) _____? Have they
inherited a (4) _____ from a parent, or is it because of their (5) _____?
Do they have a nerve cell that results in a (6) _____ to decision making without
(7) _____? Or is the (8) _____ we all feel in life too strong?

READING Risk-takers: Who are they? 🇬🇧

Before you read

**Imagine a typical risk-taker. Write down notes about the person's age,
appearance, character, gender, job, free-time activities, and social life.
Then compare notes with a partner.**

Global reading

■ **SUMMARIZING** ▒▒▒▒▒

Summarizing the key points in a text enables you to gain a good understanding of the content.
Follow these steps for making effective summaries:

1 Skim-read the text to get an idea of the topic.

2 Reread the text more carefully. Divide it into sections and take notes of the main points and
   supporting evidence/facts.

3 Using your notes, write a thesis statement. This is one sentence which summarizes the main
   argument in the text. Include the writer's name and the article date, e.g., *Smith (2013) says …*

4 Write your summary. Start with the thesis statement, followed by supporting ideas/evidence. Link
   these ideas appropriately. Be objective and stick to what the writer said, but use your own words.

1 **Skim-read the research paper, *Risk-takers: Who are they?* on pages 40–41
   by Dr. Charlie Wittman, on why people take risks. Check the possible causes
   that he discusses.**

   1 ☐ Social background   4 ☐ Age
   2 ☐ Genetic factors   5 ☐ Work experience
   3 ☐ Brain chemicals   6 ☐ Gender

2 **Read *Risk-takers: Who are they?* in more detail and take notes on the main
   idea and the supporting evidence and ideas. Compare notes with a partner.**

3 **Use your notes to help you choose the most appropriate thesis statement.
   Why are the others not appropriate?**

   1 Wittman (2012) believes that people are willing to take more risks because
      of genes they inherit from their parents.
   2 Wittman (2012) suggests that age, gender, brain, and biological makeup
      can all help to determine whether a person is a risk-taker.
   3 Wittman (2012) states that there is a stronger case for biological reasons
      determining risk-taking than psychological reasons.

Critical thinking skill

1 **Read *Risk-takers: Who are they?* and your notes again and find the source for each piece of information.**

    1 Risk-takers have fewer dopamine receptors in their nerve cells.
    2 Sensation-seeking is a personality trait which causes you to look for excitement.
    3 The sensation-seeking trait can be passed on to children.
    4 Our pre-frontal cortex may not fully develop until as late as 25.
    5 Men and women take different types of risks.
    6 Perceptions of risk are different depending on a person's past experience and familiarity with the situation he or she is in.

ASSESSING WHETHER RESEARCH SUPPORTS AN ARGUMENT

It is common for writers to use research to support their arguments in a text. When assessing cited research, ask yourself these questions:

Currency: Is the research up-to-date?

Reliability: Were the results obtained just once, or have the results been repeated? Was the research carried out by a reliable and independent organization?

Validity: Did the research include a large sample audience or a small number of people from just one or two groups? Could the results have been caused by something else?

Relevance: Is the research relevant to the argument being made? Do the results of the survey directly support the conclusions being drawn?

---

2 **Look at the research you identified in exercise 1 and answer the questions.**

    1 How is the dopamine receptor research valid?
    2 How is the sensation-seeking personality trait research relevant?
    3 How is the research showing that sensation-seeking can be passed on to children valid?
    4 How is the pre-frontal cortex research reliable?
    5 Does the research into male/female differences and perceptions of risk have currency? Is it relevant?

Developing critical thinking

Discuss these questions in a group.

1 Do you agree that young people take more risks than older people? Why or why not?
2 How do parents, schools, the government etc. try to minimize the risk that young people take in your country? Is it their responsibility to do so? Why or why not?
3 Whose responsibility is it to teach children how to calculate risk so they make safer decisions in their lives? Why? How can they do it?
4 How do you assess risk in your own life? Do you think you do this successfully, or are there things you should do differently? If so, what are they?

RISK-TAKERS: WHO ARE THEY?

By Dr Charlie Wittman 🇬🇧

[1]Jamie is a risk-taker; a 24-year-old financial accountant who spends his earnings on motorbikes and kite-surfing. Risk is something we face daily, whether it is deciding how a company should invest to ensure its future or whether to take an umbrella to work. However, some people, like Jamie, are obviously more willing to take risks than others. Biological and psychological evidence indicates that Jamie is a risk-taker because of the way his brain processes dopamine; because he is a novelty-seeker; and because he is young and male. This paper explores that evidence.

Biological reasons for risk-taking

[2] Biologists appear to have discovered a physical reason that explains why some people like Jamie are risk-takers. Dopamine is a neurotransmitter, a chemical that transmits signals between nerve cells (neurons). It is linked to the brain's reward system and is the chemical that makes us feel good, and scientists believe it to be linked to risk-taking. Our nerve cells have dopamine receptors which control the amount of dopamine that each cell receives, but not all receptors may be active. When a person has few active receptors to control the amount of dopamine that is received, a cell can become flooded, resulting in an extreme feeling of happiness.

[3] Researchers at Vanderbilt University in Nashville and Albert Einstein College of Medicine in New York asked 34 men and women to complete a questionnaire about their risk-taking to assess whether they seek new opportunities or are cautious in life. This was then followed by a brain scan using a technique called *positron emission tomography* to analyse the number of dopamine receptors that the participants had. The results of the research, reported in the *Journal of Neuroscience* (2008), were consistent with similar studies carried out with rats, and had the same outcome. It concluded that people who are risk-takers have fewer dopamine receptors than people who are not. This suggests that the rush of pleasure a risk-taker receives when a cell becomes flooded with dopamine can become addictive for some people. They therefore pursue new and exciting activities in order to try to repeat this feeling, and as a result their concern for risk becomes considerably reduced.

Psychological reasons for risk-taking

[4] Dopamine gives us a biological reason for risk-taking, but scientists believe there may be psychological reasons too. Sensation-seeking is a personality trait that describes the desire to find activities that bring us pleasure. In 1964, psychologist Marvin Zuckerman created the sensation-seeking scale, a personality test which was designed to show how much of the trait a person has. His 40-item questionnaire, still used today, was given to people who were active in seeking new activities, and to people who were more satisfied with a quiet life. From the results, he decided that there are four components of sensation-seeking. The first is *thrill and adventure seeking*; for example doing dangerous sports. The second is *experience seeking*; looking for new experiences. The third is *disinhibition*; the desire to take risks in social activities. The fourth is *boredom susceptibility*; a low tolerance of boredom. While risk-taking is not a trait in itself, it is very much associated with sensation-seeking, as a high sensation-seeker does not appraise risk in the same way that a low sensation-seeker does. A desire to achieve pleasure means that there is a greater willingness to take more risks.

[5] Studies of identical twins have been carried out to determine whether sensation-seeking is a result of genes or our environment. Pairs of twins who had grown up together and pairs of twins who had grown up apart were studied (Zuckerman, 2007). The study determined that 60% of the sensation-seeking trait can be determined by genes, showing just how influential genes are in risk-taking. This is higher than many other traits, which usually range from 30–50%, suggesting that the sensation-seeking trait, and a tendency towards risk-taking, can in fact be inherited.

Age and risk-taking

[6] Age is also relevant to the area of risk-taking. When we look at the actions of some young people, they seem to have been done with a clear disregard for safety. It now appears there may be neurological reasons for this. Dr Jay Giedd from the National Institute of Mental Health in the U.S. (2008) conducted a study which involved scanning the brains of 145 children every two years for ten years using an MRI (magnetic resonance image) scanner. The results showed that the area of the brain that sits just behind the forehead—the pre-frontal cortex—does not fully develop until as late as 25. This part of the brain is known to control the way we organise, plan, make judgments, and reason, so it is essential for calculating risk. If teenagers and young adults are dependent on a part of their brain which is not fully formed until their mid-20s, it is logical that they will sometimes miscalculate and therefore take more risks.

Gender and risk-taking

[7] It may be believed that Jamie, the risk-taker introduced at the beginning of this paper, takes risks simply because he is male, assuming that fewer women are risk-takers. But according to recent research by Columbia Business School in the U.S. (2011), gender seems to have an effect on the type of risk-taking that takes place and not whether it actually occurs. The research found that financial risks are more typical of men whereas social risks, such as giving a controversial opinion in public or making a significant career change, are more representative of women. These differences may be related to a person's perception of how risky an action is. The researchers suggest that when you are less familiar with a situation, you are more likely to perceive it as risky. They believe that men and women perceive situations differently, possibly because of their different life experiences affected by their gender. While Jamie may not be involved in risky behaviour as a direct result of being male, his gender and life experiences to date could have impacted on his choice of career, allowing him to take risks in a situation in which he does not perceive himself to be doing so.

Conclusion

[8] There has been much research that examines risk-taking and why different people behave differently. The research presented in this paper indicates that there are both biological and psychological explanations as to why people like Jamie may choose to take more risks than others. However, none of these explanations are definitive. It is possible that the brain's reward system, a person's sensation-seeking character, age, and gender all impact on risk-taking behaviour.

ACADEMIC KEYWORDS		
pursue	(v)	/pər'su/
psychological	(adj)	/ˌsaɪkə'lɑdʒɪk(ə)l/
tolerance	(n)	/'tɑlərəns/

Sources

Figner, B. & Weber, E.U. (2011). Who takes risks and why? Determinants of risk-taking, *Current Directions in Psychological Science*, 20 (4), 211–216.

Giedd, J.N. (2008). The Teen Brain: Insights from Neuroimaging, *The Journal of Adolescent Health*, 42 (4), 335–543.

Zald, D.H. et al. (2008). Midbrain dopamine receptor availability is inversely associated with novelty-seeking, *The Journal of Neuroscience*, 28 (53).

Zuckerman, M. (1964). Development of a sensation-seeking scale, *The Journal of Consulting Psychology*, 28 (6), 477–782.

Zuckerman, M. (2007). *Sensation Seeking and Risky Behavior*, Washington, DC, American Psychological Association.

Language development

ADJECTIVE + PREPOSITION COLLOCATIONS

Collocations consist of two or more words which are commonly used together. There are many adjective + preposition collocations in English.

*Some people are obviously more **willing to** take risks than others.*

*Technology **capable of** scanning the brain in detail was used in the study.*

Collocations have to be learned individually as there are generally few patterns. When reading in English, try to notice adjective + preposition collocations to help you.

1 **Complete the sentences with an appropriate preposition in the box. Some prepositions are used more than once.**

| for | in | of | on | to | with |

1 Sensation-seekers are generally more active _____ finding new activities.

2 Young people are so dependent _____ their parents for money that they cannot afford to take financial risks.

3 Young people who take risks while driving are not representative _____ all young drivers.

4 Some people are not satisfied _____ their lives and so take risks to create excitement.

5 Men being greater risk-takers is consistent _____ most people's perceptions.

6 Men are more likely to be involved _____ risky sports than women.

7 People are more willing _____ take risks today than they were a hundred years ago.

8 People do not want to take risks related _____ money at the moment.

9 Doing something without thinking about the consequences is typical _____ young people.

10 If a rule is not relevant _____ you, you do not need to follow it.

11 Understanding statistics is essential _____ risk managers.

12 Public safety announcements are influential _____ stopping people from taking risks.

2 **Find the adjectives and prepositions in *Risk-takers: Who are they?* to check your answers in exercise 1.**

3 **Discuss the sentences in exercise 1 with a partner. Do you agree or disagree with them? Why or why not?**

INFINITIVE PHRASES

The infinitive is the form of the verb that is used with *to* after certain verbs (e.g., *seem, want*) and adjectives; and modal verbs without *to* (e.g., *could, must*).

*Risk-taking can **result** in success or failure, but if you want **to achieve** something, then it is usually necessary **to take** some kind of risk.*

There are other forms of the infinitive which can change the meaning of a sentence:

Perfect infinitive Suggests the action took place before the time we are talking about *to have* + past participle	*Biologists appear **to have discovered** a physical reason that explains why some people are risk-takers.*
Continuous infinitive Suggests the action is in progress around the time we are talking about *to be* + *–ing* verb	*Young people seem **to be taking** more risks these days.*
Passive infinitive Focuses on the action and not the person doing the action *to be* + past participle	*Scientists believe it **to be linked** to risk-taking.*

The infinitive forms above can be used with modal verbs, but there is no *to* before the infinitive verb.

*His genes **may have caused** his reckless behaviour as a teen.* (modal + *have* + past participle)

*We **should be trying** to reduce risk-taking among young people.* (modal + continuous infinitive)

*His research suggests that the sensation-seeking trait **can** in fact **be inherited**.* (modal + passive infinitive)

1 What is the difference in meaning between the sentences in each pair?

1 Some adults appear to take regular risks.
  Some adults appear to have taken regular risks.

2 Risky behavior is likely to be causing unnecessary accidents.
  Risky behavior is likely to have caused unnecessary accidents.

3 Many people would like to take more risks in life.
  Many people would like to have taken more risks in life.

4 Without risk-taking, humans would not have achieved so much.
  Without risk-taking, so much would not have been achieved.

2 Complete the text with the perfect, continuous, or passive infinitive form of the verbs in parentheses.

COMMENTS

Parents these days seem (1) _____ (*protect*) their children more than ever before. And yet the truth is that children must (2) _____ (*give*) the opportunity to take risks in order to aid their development. By the time a child becomes an adult, he/she needs (3) _____ (*learn*) how to deal with the success and failure associated with risk-taking, as these skills will (4) _____ (*need*) in the adult world. It's a real shame that children today appear (5) _____ (*miss out*) on typical childhood activities such as tree climbing because of their parents' fear of injury, especially as many of those parents are likely (6) _____ (*enjoy*) such activities when they were growing up.

WRITING Summary writing

You are going to learn about ways in which you can avoid plagiarizing someone else's work when you write academic texts. You are then going to employ these techniques when writing a summary of a research paper.

Writing skill

AVOIDING PLAGIARISM

Plagiarism is copying someone's work so that it appears to be your own. If you are suspected of plagiarism, your work will usually be disqualified. When you include other people's ideas in your writing, make sure you avoid plagiarism.

- Give credit to the author by including his/her name and the date of the work.

  Dr. Atkins (2012) claims that…

- Put any phrases you take from a text between quotation marks.

  Wittman (2012) suggests that "peer pressure is influential in risky behavior."

- Paraphrase the author's ideas. This means putting them completely into your own words. Changing one or two words is not enough.

  Original statement: *Gluckman (2014): "Peer pressure affects how teenagers act."*

  Gluckman (2014) suggests that peer pressure affects how teenagers act. ✗

  Gluckman (2014) suggests that a young person's actions may be affected by friends who encourage him/her to act in a certain way. ✓

- If you want to reference an author's work that you have read in another author's work, you must include both names and dates.

  Stirling (as cited in Roberts, 2010) says that risk-taking among teenagers is not as high as many people believe.

- Include a full bibliography at the end of your text. Order items alphabetically by author's surname.

1 **Read the following excerpt of a 2013 essay by professor of sociology Dr. Bauman. What is the topic?**

Peer pressure may be having an effect on today's teenage drivers. In a study at Temple University, teenagers, students, and adults had to decide whether to stop at yellow lights or drive through them in a video game. When they believed that two same-sex friends were watching them in the next room, the teenagers drove through 40% more yellow lights, which resulted in 60% more crashes. Such results help to explain the higher number of car accidents among this age group.

2 **Read the paragraph again and take notes on the key points. Then, using your notes, write a thesis statement to summarize the main idea.**

3 **Look at the summary of the essay excerpt below. How does it plagiarize the essay?**

Peer pressure may be having an impact on teenage drivers today. In a study, young drivers drove through 40% more yellow lights in a video game when they thought their friends were watching. These results can explain why teenagers have a higher number of accidents.

4 **Write a two- or three-line summary of the excerpt in your own words, but giving credit to the author. Use your notes to help you write your summary. Do not look at the original essay excerpt again to avoid copying the author's words.**

WRITING TASK

You are going to write a summary of *Risk-takers: Who are they?*

Read the summary of an academic paper that has been written by a university student. Underline any adjective + preposition collocations and circle examples of perfect, continuous, and passive infinitives. Decide whether the summary has been sourced appropriately.

Audience:	a teacher and students
Context:	a summary of a research paper
Purpose:	develop summary writing skills

In her article "The need to learn risk" (2013), which can be found in the *Journal of Risk Literacy* (Vol. 2, Issue 4), Patricia Hughes argues that risk literacy is essential in our daily lives and therefore should be studied in schools in order to help young people to calculate risk better, suggesting ways in which risk literacy could be taught. To support her argument, Hughes provides evidence that risk literacy education has been successful among 16-year-olds. One hundred 16-year-olds were involved in her study, which required them to make decisions about how to save or invest money both prior and subsequent to receiving lessons on statistics. The teenagers appeared to have been more successful in making decisions based on calculated risk after their lessons, which prompted Hughes to say that "secondary schools should be doing more to teach risk literacy in math lessons."

BRAINSTORM

On page 38 you read tips for writing a summary of the key points in a text. Can you remember the steps to take when doing this?

Step 1:   Step 3:

Step 2:   Step 4:

PLAN

Look at the thesis statement you chose and the notes you created on *Risk-takers: Who are they?* on page 38. Plan a summary of this research paper by choosing what to include and placing these items into an appropriate order. Use the example summary above to help you.

WRITE

Write your summary in around 300 words. Make sure you avoid plagiarism by citing sources, paraphrasing, and using direct quotes. Use adjective + preposition collocations and infinitive forms where appropriate.

SHARE

Exchange your summary with a partner. Read the checklist below and give feedback to your partner.
- Has your partner summarized the text objectively?
- Has your partner cited sources?
- Has your partner paraphrased appropriately?
- Has your partner included a thesis statement and supporting ideas?

REWRITE AND EDIT

Consider your partner's comments and rewrite your summary.

STUDY SKILLS Evaluating online sources

Getting started

Discuss these questions with a partner.

1 What's your favorite website for accessing information for school/college? What are its benefits and limitations?
2 Is it easier to access information online or in printed material? Why? Think of three reasons.
3 How is printed material better than online material? Think of three advantages.

Scenario

Read the scenario and think about what Liliana did right and what she did wrong.

Consider it

Read the tips about evaluating online sources. Which strategies do you already use? Which strategies do you think would be useful for you to try? Why?

1 **Be objective.** Do not search only for information that supports your opinion. Find information that gives different views so you can provide balanced information.
2 **Source appropriate websites.** Think about the type of text you are writing and look for websites that are relevant to that. When writing an academic text, you will find that online journals, newspaper reports of research, and other academic sites are most helpful.
3 **Be critical.** Do not assume that everything you read is true. Check that information is up-to-date and of good quality. Do statistics or research come from a reliable source? Can they be confirmed elsewhere? Avoid anonymous websites.
4 **Check that the author is credible.** Websites that include information about the author are likely to be more credible than those that do not. Try to find out about the author's experience, background, and reputation. If the author is biased, you may not be able to trust his/her information.
5 **Source information appropriate to the topic.** Make sure that the information you choose to use addresses the area of the topic that you are writing about. Avoid information that will take you away from this topic.
6 **Note down web addresses.** Keep a record of any websites you want to revisit or source in your essay as you do your research. You may not find them again if you do not bookmark them or note them down, and this will make it difficult to evaluate them or source them later in your writing.

Over to you

Discuss these questions with a partner.

1 What other strategies do you think are useful when doing Internet research? Think of two.
2 How do you usually organize your online research?
3 Do you know of any useful web programs or apps that can help you to organize your studies? Describe them.

Liliana's tutor asked her to write an essay on whether young people should not be allowed to drive until the age of 21 due to their risky behavior.

Liliana used a search engine to find information about the topic and read the first ten websites listed. Half of these were academic websites, two were driving websites, one was a campaign website, and two were blogs. Each one gave Liliana some ideas about the topic and all agreed with her opinion that the driving age should be increased. She made notes of the key points and then saved the web addresses in her bookmarks.

In her essay, Liliana used this information to argue her point, carefully sourcing it where possible; one of the web pages she found had no author listed, and the blog comments were anonymous, so she could not source those. She included some research done by a university that supported her opinion, and statistics from a road safety campaign website.

READING	Identifying different perspectives
CRITICAL THINKING	Recognizing trends and patterns
LANGUAGE DEVELOPMENT	Prepositional phrases
	Impersonal report structures
WRITING	Hedging

Discussion point

Discuss these questions with a partner.

1 Are you from the city or the countryside? Do you like where you live? Why or why not?
2 What are the advantages and disadvantages of living in a city? Think of at least three of each.
3 What are some of the problems that exist in your nearest city? How do you think they could be solved?

Vocabulary preview

1 Match the first half of each definition with the second half.

1   To *rehouse* someone means to
2   *Non-governmental organizations* (NGOs)
3   *Tenancy rights* are
4   *Urbanization* describes
5   A *settlement* is a place where
6   *Infrastructure* describes
7   *Sustainable* resources are
8   A *migrant* is a person who

a   the process where a city grows because people move there.
b   travels to another place or country in order to find work.
c   move someone to a different home.
d   the legal rights you have to use a piece of land or house.
e   the systems within a place or area, e.g., roads, electricity network.
f   people come to live permanently.
g   are groups that work with governments in the field of development.
h   available for a long time and do not damage the environment.

2 Why are the following important for a growing city? Which is most important?

> infrastructure   migrant workers   sustainable resources   tenancy rights

READING Solving the problem of informal settlements 🇬🇧

Before you read

Look at the picture below and answer the questions.

1   Why do people live in informal settlements like this? Think of three reasons.
2   What do you think life is like for them? What reasons can you give for this?
3   What name is given to informal settlements like this and the people who live in them in your language? Do you know any other names for them in English?

Global reading

> **IDENTIFYING DIFFERENT PERSPECTIVES**
>
> An analysis of an idea, project, case study, etc. is likely to consider and reference the perspectives of all the groups of people involved, whether this is done explicitly or implicitly. For example, the paper on pages 50–51 looks at informal settlements and includes the viewpoints of various groups involved in those communities.
>
> When reading such a text, it is important to identify the different perspectives to get a much fuller understanding of the issues involved and assess the quality of the analysis. As you read, underline the groups of people that are mentioned and focus on what the writer says about each.

1 Read a paper by Kamal Rajan, a student intern with an NGO, entitled *Solving the problem of informal settlements* on pages 50–51. What is the difference between rehousing people and upgrading settlements?

2 Underline the different groups of people mentioned in the text.

3 Read the paper again and make notes in a table similar to the one below that may reflect each group's perspective on rehousing and upgrading.

	Rehousing	Settlement upgrading
Informal community residents		
Governments		
Other city residents		
NGOs		

4 **Decide whether these occur with the rehousing of residents (R), the upgrading of existing communities (U), or both (B).**

1 A more secure home _____
2 Mental well-being _____
3 Greater employment opportunities _____
4 City's infrastructure stretched _____
5 Residents join mainstream society _____
6 Government and community work together _____

Critical thinking skill

■ RECOGNIZING TRENDS AND PATTERNS ■

Many academic texts include statistical information. Statistics may describe a static figure, or they may describe a trend or pattern. A trend is a gradual change or development, whereas a pattern is a series of repeated events or actions that tell us how things normally happen.

Over 50% of people live in cities. (= static figure)

Unemployment has risen by 3%. (= trend)

Rent prices have increased to an average of $200 per month. (= trend)

Many families earn just a few dollars each day. (= pattern)

Several hundred people move to the city each month. (= pattern)

When we are not sure about the exact figures, we use vague language with phrases such as *approximately, just over, just under, more than, almost, just, about.*

This number is expected to reach almost 1.5 billion.

Estimated to cost just over $1.2 billion, …

1 **Complete the sentences with a number from the text.**

1 There will be _____ people living in cities in 2030, up from _____ in 2008.
2 _____ people live in informal settlements today.
3 _____ more people are expected to move to informal settlements before the end of the decade.
4 _____% of people are estimated to earn less than $30 a month in Kibera.
5 _____% of young people are said to be out of work in Kibera.
6 _____% of jobs are thought to be created by the informal economy.
7 The Mumbai recycling industry has a value of £_____.
8 The global population is expected to grow by _____ by 2030.

2 **Look at the statistics in exercise 1. Which statistics represent a trend? Which represent a pattern? Which are static figures?**

Developing critical thinking

Discuss these questions in a group.

1 What conclusions does the author make? Is he exact about his conclusions or is he vague? How do you know?
2 Do you agree with the author's conclusions? Why or why not?
3 What do you think governments should do to prepare for future migration from rural to urban areas?

ACADEMIC KEYWORDS

conditions	(pl n)	/kən'dɪʃ(ə)nz/
generate	(v)	/'dʒenə,reɪt/
unstable	(adj)	/ʌn'steɪb(ə)l/

SOLVING THE PROBLEM OF INFORMAL SETTLEMENTS

By Kamal Rajan

[1] It is predicted that by 2030, five billion people will be living in urban areas, up from 3.3billion in 2008, as people seek to improve their economic situations and gain better access to services (UNFPA, 2007). While urbanization is generally considered to be a key indicator in development, it tends to bring with it a wider level of social inequality and a more uneven distribution of wealth, inevitably resulting in informal settlements and the poverty that exists within them. Nearly one billion people are said to currently live in these settlements, also known as slums, shanty towns, or favelas. That is one in every seven people in the world living in unsanitary conditions in cheap, unsafe housing built on land with no secure tenancy rights. This number is on the increase and expected to reach almost 1.5 billion before 2020 (UN-HABITAT, 2010). Governments and organizations are therefore seeking solutions to today's problems in order to prepare for the future. One of two main approaches is generally adopted: rehousing residents to another area with improved facilities, or upgrading the facilities in existing settlements. This paper assesses rehousing and its impact on wealth, health, and the environment.

IMPACT ON WEALTH

[2] In 2009 the Kenyan government, with the aid of UN-HABITAT, started a scheme to rehouse the residents of the Kibera settlement, one of Africa's largest informal settlements built on unstable land. Estimated to cost $1.2 billion, this scheme involves the building of low-rent housing around the city to provide safe accommodation, running water, and power to the thousands of people who live there. On the face of it, this scheme will provide many financial benefits for the city. First, it will help tackle the enduring poverty that exists in informal communities, which in turn will increase the city's economy as people gain formal employment and pay taxes. Governments will reclaim the land and nearby city residents will no longer feel that informal settlements impact on the value of their own homes.

[3] However, it is possible that the scheme in Kibera will suffer from a problem that similar projects have experienced in the past—residents choosing to return to their old community (Patel, 2011). One reason for this is cost. The new accommodation in Kibera may appear cheap to the outside world at $10 a month, but for the 60% of the Kibera population living on $1 a day and for the 80% of Kiberan youth who are unemployed (International Labour Organization, 2011), it may still be prohibitively expensive. As a result, some residents may choose to stay in the settlement and rent out their new home to middle-class families at a profit.

4 In terms of employment, rehousing takes people away from work and their opportunities to earn money. Informal settlements are lively communities with thriving, albeit informal (i.e., not taxed), economies full of small businesses and micro-entrepreneurs—people who have become inventive in response to extreme living conditions. It is said that around 85% of all new employment around the world is generated within informal economies (UN-HABITAT, 2010), emphasising just how important these settlements are to the people who live in them.

IMPACT ON HEALTH

5 Rehousing can reduce the disease and poor health common in informal communities due to poor sanitation. However, it can also separate people from their family and friends, which may have a negative impact on their psychological health. This is one reason why some governments and NGOs are in favour of investing their resources on upgrading existing settlements rather than moving people away from their existing lives. One such project was undertaken by the government of Colombia, who wanted to improve the infrastructure in the poor district of Medellin. It invested $6.7 million in a giant escalator to make it easier for people to walk up and down the side of the mountain from their homes to their work (Tamayo, 2011).

IMPACT ON THE ENVIRONMENT

6 In informal settlements, nothing is wasted and recycling is a part of everyday life. By moving residents to new housing, the city risks putting additional strain on its infrastructure and finite resources, such as electricity for lighting. In Dharavi, one of the largest informal settlements in India, recycling has played an even bigger role in the life of its people. Thousands of small businesses are in operation with over 250,000 people involved, taking the 4,000 tonnes of waste from Mumbai each day and recycling it. It is estimated that the industry could be worth as much as £700 million a year (MacDougall, 2007). In the event of this industry disappearing, Mumbai citizens could be quite literally knee-deep in waste without a very large increase in government investment in infrastructure.

LAND RIGHTS

7 Rehousing residents is by no means a redundant approach. In Kibera, where the land is dangerous to build on, or in cases where the government cannot obtain the land rights, rehousing may be the most appropriate choice of action. There are success stories, an example being Alagados in Brazil, where 984 families were moved into single-family homes over five years, after which over 80% of the residents had access to water, electricity, sewage facilities, and garbage collection (Cities Alliance, 2008). The families were given new homes and training in basic life skills, but most importantly they were consulted throughout the process to ensure they had a say in their new community.

CONCLUSION

8 Informal settlement rehousing projects appear to have met with a mixed degree of success. They offer clean, comfortable accommodation, but they can also take people away from their families, employment, and the community. In light of this, it seems that rehousing is the most effective option when settlements are situated on unstable land or land without rights. In addition, when rehousing people it is important that those people are involved in the planning process to ensure that new housing is affordable and a successful community is created. With an estimated growth of two billion in the global population by 2030 (UN-HABITAT, 2010), it is vital that cities address this issue today in order to prepare for the future.

SOURCES

Cities Alliance. (2008). Alagados: The story of integrated slum upgrading in Salvador (Bahia), retrieved 21 June 2012 from http://www.citiesalliance.org.
International Labour Organization, 2011. From the depths of an African Shanty town, a nascent youth employment monement grows, retrieved 23 June 2012 from http://www.ilo.org/global/about-the-ilo/newsroom/features/WCMS_170345/lang-en/index.htm.
MacDougall, D. (2007). Waste not want not in the £700 million slum, *Guardian*, retrieved 30 June 2007 from http://www.guardian.co.uk/environment/2007/mar/04/india.recycling.
Patel, N. (2011). Battle over Mumbai's slums, retrieved 15 June 2012 from http://www.guardian.co.uk/global-development/poverty-matters/2011/mar/11/mumbai-slums-developers-profits-residents.

Tamayo, A. (2011). Colombian city opens giant outdoor escalator, retrieved 22 June 2012 from http://digitaljournal.com/article/316831.
United Nations. (2003). The challenge of the slums, retrieved 22 June 2012 from http://www.unhabitat.org.
UN-HABITAT. (2007). Slum dwellers to double by 2030, retrieved 25 June 2012 from http://www.unhabitat.org
UN-HABITAT. (2010). State of the world's cities report 2010–2011, retrieved 2 July 2012 from http://www.unhabitat.org.
UNFPA. (2007). Unleashing the potential of urban growth: State of World Population, http://www.unfpa.org/public/publications/pid/408.

Language development

PREPOSITIONAL PHRASES

Prepositional phrases begin with a preposition and end with either a noun, pronoun, gerund, or noun clause (cf. p. 73).

preposition + noun	*down the side of a mountain*
preposition + pronoun	*with them*
preposition + gerund	*by rehousing residents*
preposition + noun clause	*with what they have*

Prepositional phrases can act as an adjective and describe a noun or pronoun. They tell us which one, whose, what kind, or how many. In this sentence it tells us what kind of land:

*One in every seven people lives in unsafe housing built on land **with no secure tenancy rights**.*

Prepositional phrases can also act as an adverb and modify a verb or adjective. They tell us how, where, when, or why. In this sentence it tells us why:

*Their aim is to drive economic development **with a view to** bringing residents into the mainstream of society.*

Many of them are set phrases, e.g., *in the end, without a doubt, in conclusion.* Some begin and end with a preposition, e.g., *with a view to, at a rate of, on the edge of.*

***Without a doubt**, people in urban areas have better access to education.*

*People are moving to the city **at a rate of** hundreds a day.*

1 **Find and underline the prepositional phrases in the box in *Solving the problem of informal settlements.***

> by no means   in favour of   in light of   in response to
> in terms of   in the event of   on the face of it   on the increase

2 **Complete the text with the prepositional phrases.**

(1) _____, city life seems hectic, stressful, and expensive. But if we look closer, we can see that urban living is (2) _____ all negative. The majority of people move to the city (3) _____ a desire or the need to improve their economic situation. (4) _____ jobs and education, urban areas provide far greater opportunities for development, which is why many families are (5) _____ making such a huge change to their lives. (6) _____ a serious illness or accident, it is good to know that there are facilities nearby that can provide good medical care, and there are far greater entertainment facilities in the city than in the countryside.

With all this in mind, it is not hard to understand why the numbers of city migrants are (7) _____ as more people search for these kinds of facilities. (8) _____ the huge advantages, you could say that tolerating the few disadvantages above is really not so bad.

3 Match the underlined phrases with their definitions a–e.

1   The best way to experience life in [city name] is <u>by</u> …
2   <u>Contrary to</u> 20 years ago, [city name] …
3   <u>With a view to</u> improving life in [city name], the local government should …
4   Life in [city name] would also be improved <u>with the aid of</u> …
5   <u>In relation to</u> entertainment in [city name], you …

a   in the hope of
b   concerning
c   completely different/opposite to
d   with the method of
e   with help from

4 Think about a city you know well and complete the sentences in exercise 3 with your own ideas.

IMPERSONAL REPORT STRUCTURES

Impersonal report structures are very common in academic English and are often used to describe general beliefs or to present widely accepted information that does not have a specific source. They are also used when the person who did the action is unknown or unimportant. There are three common structures:

- *It* + passive + *that* + clause (*It is believed that migration to cities is on the increase.*)
- Subject + passive + *to* + infinitive (*Migration to cities is believed to be on the increase.*)
- *There* + passive + *to* + infinitive (*There is believed to be an increase in migration to cities.*)

1 Rewrite each sentence, starting with the words in parentheses. Use an impersonal report structure.

1   We know that people are unable to find work in rural areas. (It …)
2   People suppose that living in a city brings more employment opportunities. (Living in a city …)
3   They think that there is greater access to schooling. (There …)
4   People believe that transport is much better in the city. (It …)
5   We estimate that there are 70 million people moving to cities each year. (There …)
6   Some people allege that urban life is worse for migrants. (Urban life …)
7   Other people claim that this is not true and rural life is far worse. (It …)
8   We say that urbanization is necessary for a country to develop. (Urbanization …)

2 What kind of reputation does your city/nearest city have? Complete the sentences with your own ideas about what people believe is true.

1   It is said that …
2   There is believed to be …
3   It is claimed that the people …
4   The city area is thought to …
5   In the future it is expected to …

3 Work with a partner and tell each other what you have written, giving explanations. Is the reputation you describe fair?

WRITING An argumentative essay

You are going to learn about ways to sound more vague in your writing when presenting figures, arguments, or opinions. You are then going to use this language when writing an argumentative essay.

Writing skill

HEDGING

Academic texts will present information as fact only when it can be supported by sufficient indisputable evidence. Often a writer does not have enough access to such evidence and therefore uses vague—hedging—language to ensure the information is presented fairly and accurately. Compare these sentences:

*The industry **is worth** as much as £700m a year.*

*The industry **could be worth** as much as £700m a year.*

*Rehousing projects **have met** with a mixed degree of success.*

*Rehousing projects **appear to have met** with a mixed degree of success.*

Hedging language includes certain verbs (e.g., *assume, appear*); modal verbs of probability (e.g., *could, might*); adverbs of frequency (e.g., *often, sometimes*); adverbs of probability (e.g., *definitely, probably*); and determiners (e.g., *some*).

1 Underline the hedging language in each sentence.

   1 Generally speaking, innovation in informal settlements indicates a desire for self-improvement.

   2 The best ideas appear to be those developed within the community and are likely to involve collaboration.

   3 New products invented in an informal settlement tend to be made with recycled resources, which suggests they are environmentally friendly.

   4 In some cases, business leaders have examined innovation in slums because they think their organizations may succeed better as a result.

2 Read the article about an innovative type of tourism entitled *City tours, but not as you know them*. Does the writer present information as fact, or does she use hedging language? Do you think the writer is correct to do this?

City tours, but not as you know them

A different kind of city tour is helping people to understand how others live. Nicknamed "slum tours," they involve trips to the poorest areas and are becoming popular in cities around the world. Visitors who go on such a tour learn about the challenges that people who live there face, as well as discover the positive elements that exist, such as creativity and innovation. Some tour guides employ people from the settlements so the community benefits, and as people become more aware of the life in these communities, they will help more. This tourism is not without controversy, however, as people believe it exploits residents of the settlement. They also say that tourists are not interested in helping residents but just want to satisfy a curiosity, and that the only people who benefit are the tour guides.

3 Rewrite the article and make it fairer and more accurate by adding hedging language where appropriate.

A different kind of tourism appears to be helping people to understand how others live.

WRITING TASK

You are going to write an argumentative essay entitled *Slum tourism: Positive or detrimental?*

Read part of an argumentative essay written by a university student assessing the benefits and disadvantages of slum tourism. Underline the impersonal structures and circle hedging language.

Audience:	a teacher and students
Context:	a critical analysis
Purpose:	develop arguments

The key advantage of slum tourism is thought to be the understanding that tourists gain about the complexities of life in an informal settlement. Visitors can learn not only about the problems that exist within these communities, but also about the supportive community within which the residents live. This could lead to a greater understanding of how society should work together to develop these areas and improve living standards. On the other hand, it is believed that some visitors are not interested in understanding the issues but are instead visiting out of a sense of curiosity. This is unlikely to result in any kind of long-term advantage for the people that agree to be observed, and suggests that these tours are not helpful.

BRAINSTORM

Read *City tours, but not as you know them* again. Think about the effects of slum tourism on the people involved and complete the table with potential advantages and disadvantages. Use the ideas in the article to help you.

	Advantages	Disadvantages
The tourists		
The residents		
The tour company		
Society as a whole		

PLAN

Plan your essay. Prepare to write five paragraphs that include an introduction with a thesis statement, the advantages, the drawbacks, and a conclusion.

WRITE

Write your essay in around 300 words. Include impersonal structures and hedging language where appropriate to give your essay a suitable tone. Try to include a variety of prepositional phrases.

SHARE

Exchange your essay with a partner. Read the checklist below and give feedback to your partner.
- Does your partner give a balanced viewpoint, including both benefits and drawbacks?
- Does your partner's writing have an appropriate tone—i.e., does he/she use impersonal structures? Does he/she use hedging language?
- Does your partner include a variety of prepositional phrases?

REWRITE AND EDIT

Consider your partner's comments and rewrite your essay.

Internal consistency

by Stella Cottrell

Clarity and internal consistency

One important aspect of presenting a clear authorial position is creating a consistent argument, so that all parts of the line of reasoning contribute to the conclusion. Nothing then contradicts or undermines the main message. Inconsistencies make an argument hard to follow, leaving the audience uncertain about what the author is trying to persuade them to believe.

Example 1

Apples are good for your teeth. Acid corrodes. Apples consist mainly of acid so they can't be good for teeth.

Here, the message lacks internal consistency. The reader is left wondering whether apples are good for your teeth or not.

Including opposing arguments

A strong line of reasoning will usually give consideration to alternative points of view, including those that appear to contradict the main argument. A good argument manages such apparent contradiction by:

- making it clear throughout the line of reasoning what position it wants the audience to take;
- making it clear when it is introducing an alternative point of view;
- counter arguments to show why the alternative point of view is less convincing;
- resolving any apparent contradictions by showing how the main argument holds true.

Example 2

Apples are better for your teeth than refined sugar snacks. Some people argue that apples are an acid and that acid damages tooth enamel. However, any food, if left on the teeth, is bad for them. Refined sugars are particularly damaging to teeth. Compared with the sugary snacks most people eat, apples provide a more beneficial alternative and have long been recommended by dentists.

Here, the argument is internally consistent: *apples are better for your teeth than refined sugar products.* All the reasons support this. The opposing view (that acids corrode teeth) is included but its importance is minimised.

It is worth noting that the main argument is strong partly because it is worded in a more tentative way so that it is easier to defend. It is easier to argue that something is 'more beneficial than …' rather than making an absolute statement such as 'Apples are good …', which may not hold true in every circumstance.

Precision

The example above demonstrates that arguments may need to be very precisely worded. Imprecise wording is a common cause of inconsistency, as in the example below.

Example 3

Apples are good for your teeth and have long been recommended by dentists. It may seem strange that this is the case, given that apples consist of acid and acid corrodes enamel. However, the acid is relatively harmless, and certainly apples are more beneficial than alternative snacks made of refined sugar, such as sweets and cakes.

Here, the argument is relatively well structured and is more consistent than Example 1. However, it is still not a consistent argument. The author's opening statement is that 'Apples are good for your teeth.' However, by the end of the passage, the author is arguing that the acid is 'relatively harmless' and that 'apples are more beneficial than alternative snacks'. An argument about the relative benefits is not the same as the absolute statement that 'apples are good', so the message is not internally consistent.

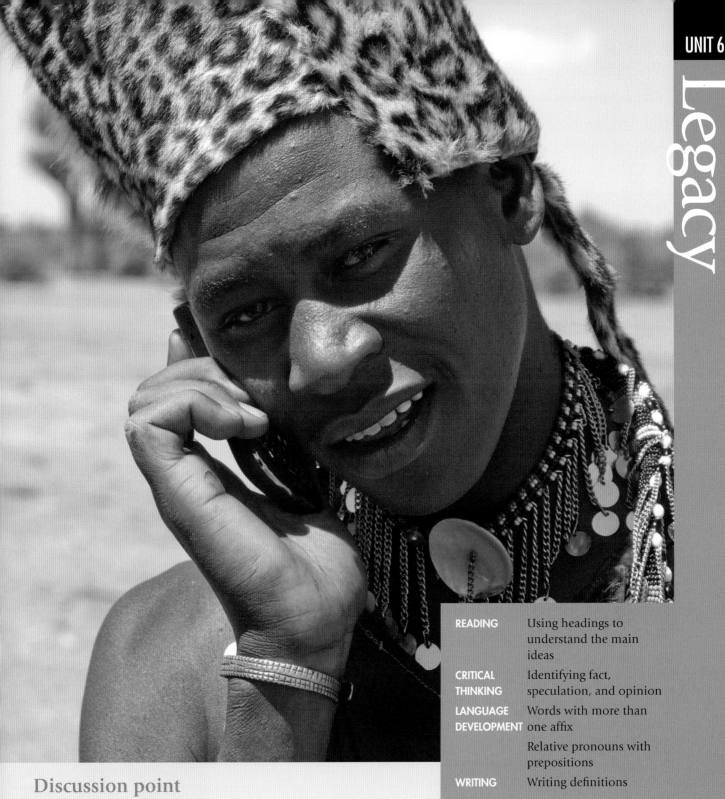

Legacy

READING	Using headings to understand the main ideas
CRITICAL THINKING	Identifying fact, speculation, and opinion
LANGUAGE DEVELOPMENT	Words with more than one affix
	Relative pronouns with prepositions
WRITING	Writing definitions

Discussion point

Discuss these questions with a partner.

1 What languages do you speak? Do your parents and grandparents speak the same languages?

2 Think about the idioms, expressions, and other ways of speaking you use in your first language (or in English). Which of these things has had the biggest influence on the way you speak?

> books family friends teachers television the Internet

3 Would the world be better off if everyone had the same first language? Make a list of advantages and drawbacks.

Vocabulary preview

Complete the sentences with the words in the box.

> document   endangered   ethnic groups   extinction
> linguist   native language   revitalize   tongue

1 _____ languages have very few speakers and may soon disappear.

2 India has hundreds of different _____, each with their own language.

3 Climate change likely caused the _____ of the dinosaurs.

4 A _____ studies language and how it works.

5 Researchers sometimes _____ endangered languages on video.

6 Your _____ is usually the one you learned as a baby.

7 To _____ an endangered language, young people must learn it.

8 The Icelandic _____ has very complex grammar and vocabulary.

READING Endangered languages: Strategies for preservation and revitalization

Before you read

**Guess the correct numbers to complete the sentences. Discuss your reasons.
(The answers are in *Endangered languages* on page 60–61.)**

1 77 / 700 / 7,000 languages are spoken around the world today.

2 15% / 40% / 67% of these languages are now endangered.

3 80% of the world's people speak only 1% / 10% / 25% of its languages.

Global reading

> ■ **USING HEADINGS TO UNDERSTAND THE MAIN IDEAS** ■
>
> Many academic texts present information in a different order than a typical
> article in a newspaper or on a website. In these cases, rather than reading
> the text from beginning to end, you can first use the headings to find the
> information you need to understand the general meaning.

1 Look at the headings in *Endangered languages*, a paper written by an
anthropology student. Predict which sections will contain the answers
to these questions.

   1 What causes a language to become endangered?

   2 How do researchers define "endangered"?

   3 How many languages are endangered?

   4 What are people doing to save endangered languages?

   5 What is lost when a language becomes extinct?

2 Skim-read *Endangered languages*. Use the headings to find answers to the
questions in exercise 1.

3 Compare answers to the questions in exercise 1 with a partner. Then read
the paper again and summarize its main points in your own words. Use your
answers in exercise 1 to help you.

Critical thinking skill

■ IDENTIFYING FACT, SPECULATION, AND OPINION ■

When reading an academic text, it is important to distinguish statements of fact from speculation and opinion. This can be difficult because writers often present speculation and opinion in a way that sounds factual.

A **fact** is something that has been proven to be true by a reliable source.

An astonishing 7,000 different languages are spoken on Earth today.

Speculation refers to statements that cannot be proven with the given facts, but which sound probable or possible based on the facts that are given. Words that indicate speculation include *likely, probably, certainly, believed to be, predict,* and modal verbs such as *could, may,* or *will.*

She isn't answering her phone, so her plane probably hasn't landed yet.

Unlike speculation, **opinion** expresses a view that cannot be proven right or wrong with facts. Other people may or may not share the same opinion.

In addition to these factors, there is the simple but profound enjoyment one takes in hearing the diversity of tongues across the world.

1 **Find these lines in *Endangered languages* and read the paragraphs where they appear. Is each line a fact, speculation, or opinion?**

1 Many of these languages also lack a system of writing. (para. 2)

2 About 1,000 people on Earth speak Koro, but as endangered languages go, this is a relatively robust figure. (para. 3)

3 Languages become endangered due to a number of interrelated factors. (para. 5)

4 We are clearly fortunate that the healer's language had not yet vanished. (para. 6)

5 The Jeru language … is thought to be closely related to the first languages ever spoken … (para. 7)

6 Technology is not to be seen as a threat, but rather an opportunity for a small language to extend its voice. (para. 9)

2 **Read *Endangered languages* again. Which of these conclusions are supported by the facts given in the paper? What are the supporting facts?**

1 The majority of the world's languages face the threat of extinction.

Not supported—Catalogue of Endangered Languages says only about 40% of languages are endangered.

2 The loss of a language hurts everyone, not only the community where the language was spoken.

3 There is little hope of saving most of the world's endangered languages.

Developing critical thinking

Discuss these questions in a group.

1 Think of three things people can do to help save endangered languages. Do you think these efforts are likely to succeed? Are they worth the cost?

2 In what ways does the writer say that the loss of a language affects everyone? Which of these points makes the strongest argument?

3 Think of two ways technology has helped endangered languages and two ways it has hurt them. Overall, do you think technology is a good thing for the world's languages?

ABSTRACT

[1] The issue of endangered languages is a growing concern, with over 3,000 languages threatened with extinction ("Why So Important?" 1). Globalization, technology, education, and cultural changes threaten the survival of these languages. The disappearance of a language is a loss not only for its speakers, but for the world at large: culture, literature, history, and scientific knowledge can vanish along with the language. Fortunately, a number of projects are now harnessing the same technology often blamed for language loss to preserve endangered languages for future generations.

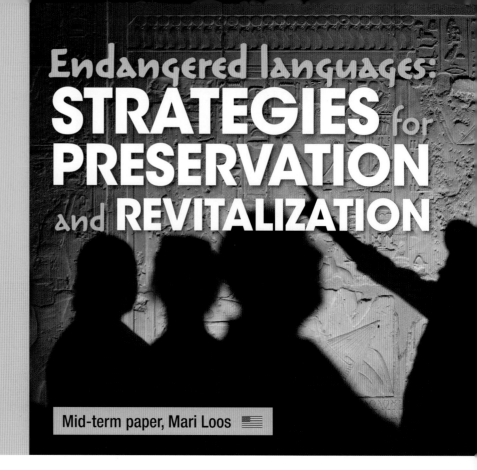

Endangered languages: STRATEGIES for PRESERVATION and REVITALIZATION

Mid-term paper, Mari Loos

ENDANGERED LANGUAGES ON THE RISE

[2] An astonishing 7,000 different languages are spoken on Earth today ("Why So Important?" 1). However, nearly 80% of the population speaks only 1% of these languages ("About Enduring Voices"), and more than 40% of the planet's languages are "endangered," meaning that there are very few living native speakers ("Why So Important?" 1). Many of these languages also lack a system of writing. When the speakers die, the language dies with them. Without action, the vast majority of these 3,000 endangered languages, many of which have not been recorded or studied at all, could soon disappear ("Why So Important?" 1).

[3] Endangered languages can be found throughout the world. Some, like the Koro language in northeastern India, have only recently become known to the outside world. About 1,000 people on Earth speak Koro (Morrison), but as endangered languages go, this is a relatively robust figure. Many languages now have fewer than 100, or even fewer than 10 speakers (Austin). The crisis is not limited to remote regions of the world. When Europeans first arrived in North America, 312 different languages were in use, of which 123 are now known to be extinct. Of the surviving languages, most speakers are grandparents and great-grandparents ("Why So Important?" 1).

WHEN AND WHY LANGUAGES BECOME ENDANGERED

[4] Different researchers offer different definitions of "endangered." The system of classification used by the Catalogue of Endangered Languages (ELCat) evaluates languages in four areas: how often the language is transmitted to the next generation, the total number of speakers, the rate at which it is losing speakers, and the situations in which it is used. Based on this data, languages are ranked on a six-point scale from "safe" to "severely endangered." The midpoint, "endangered," refers to a language with between 100 and 1,000 speakers who represent about half of the language's community or ethnic group. The language is spoken only by some parents, of whom very few teach it to their children. It is primarily used at home and is not taught in schools or used for government business ("About the Catalogue" 4–5).

[5] Languages become endangered due to a number of interrelated factors, including globalization, economics, technology, education policy, and changes in cultural attitudes. As the forces of globalization make the world more interconnected, previously isolated language communities come under pressure to participate in the larger economy, which means learning the area's majority language. In response, local schools often begin to teach the majority language instead of the local tongue. Local languages also suffer as communities adopt mobile phones and computers, most of which run on software that has been translated into only a handful of languages. This trend accelerates

ACADEMIC KEYWORDS

consequence	(n)	/ˈkɑnsəkwəns/
lack	(v)	/læk/
suggest	(v)	/səˈdʒest/

One researcher, working with a local healer in Samoa, discovered plant-based cures that led to a drug, Prostratin, which is used to treat yellow fever and may even be effective against HIV ("Why So Important?" 2). We are clearly fortunate that the healer's language had not yet vanished.

[7] In addition to these factors, there is the simple but profound enjoyment one takes in hearing the diversity of tongues across the world. Examples abound, such as the Nǀu language of Southern Africa—the "ǀ" indicates a clicking sound like the English *tsk!* This complex tongue has 74 consonants and 31 vowels. Only 10 speakers remain (Austin). The Jeru language, now spoken by fewer than 20 residents of an island in the Indian Ocean, is thought to be closely related to the first languages ever spoken and so it may shed light on how human languages first began (Austin).

REVITALIZATION EFFORTS

[8] Initiatives to revitalize endangered languages have become more numerous in recent years. These efforts tend to focus on two main areas: the documentation of endangered languages, usually with the help of the Internet and digital technology, and efforts to increase the use of endangered languages among younger speakers and in the community at large.

[9] With funding from organizations such as Google and National Geographic, linguists have traveled the world to record spoken languages and preserve them online. The American linguist David Harrison refers to these databases as "talking dictionaries." The talking dictionaries not only preserve the language for future study but also offer validation in the eyes of a community that its language matters. Harrison notes that "technology is not to be seen as a threat, but rather an opportunity for a small language to extend its voice and to reach a global audience" (*Digital Tools*). In other projects, technology has been used not to document a language but to expand

the domains in which a language is used. In the north of Canada, for example, the Inuit people worked with Microsoft® to translate the company's software into their native language, Inuktitut (*Digital Technologies*).

[10] In addition to technology, communities have started initiatives to popularize endangered languages with younger speakers. In the U.S., the Miami-Illinois language was considered extinct after its last speaker died in the 1960s, but it has recently been revived as surviving tribe members document and relearn the language. Children are now learning the language again (Google Official Blog). A similar project in the state of Oregon has spurred the popularization of the near-extinct Siletz language— it has been so successful that young people are even using the language in text messages (*Digital Technologies*). Efforts like these suggest that many endangered languages might still be saved.

as these devices connect users to the Internet. At this point, many communities undergo a cultural shift in which parents no longer value the language enough to teach it to their children ("About Enduring Voices").

WHY ENDANGERED LANGUAGES MATTER

[6] The endangerment or extinction of a language is of course a great loss for the community in which it is spoken, but it is also a loss for the world at large. A language is more than a list of words for things. It expresses concepts, values, stories, and viewpoints that are unique to its community and, in many cases, uniquely valuable to the world. Because the great majority of these languages are not written languages, a culture's oral literature is at risk when its language is endangered, as is a great deal of historical knowledge. Knowledge of the natural world and the local environment is also lost, and this can have real consequences for all of us. To cite one example, in recent years numerous valuable medicines have been found in plants tended, cultivated, and best understood by speakers of endangered languages.

SOURCES

Austin, Peter K. "Peter K Austin's Top 10 Endangered Languages." *Guardian*, Aug. 27, 2008: n. pag.

Catalogue of Endangered Languages. "About the Catalogue of Endangered Languages." Catalogue of Endangered Languages, 2012.

Catalogue of Endangered Languages. "Endangered Languages: Why So Important?" Catalogue of Endangered Languages, 2012.

Endangered Languages Project. Home page.

Enduring Voices Project. "About Enduring Voices." *National Geographic*.

Google Official Blog. "The Endangered Languages Project: Supporting language preservation through technology and collaboration." Google, June 21, 2012.

Morrison, Dan. "'Hidden' Language Found in Remote Indian Tribe." National Geographic News, Oct. 5, 2010: n. pag.

National Public Radio. *Digital Tools Help Document Vanishing Languages*. National Public Radio, Feb. 17, 2012: n. pag.

National Public Radio. *Digital Technologies Give Dying Languages New Life*. National Public Radio, Mar. 19, 2012: n. pag.

Language development

WORDS WITH MORE THAN ONE AFFIX

It is common to use more than one prefix or suffix in order to create nouns, verbs, or adjectives. For example, the word *globalization* is formed from the word *globe* by adding three suffixes.

globe + *-al* = *global* (adj.) + *-ize* = *globalize* (v.) + *-tion* = *globalization* (n.)

Similar words include *classification* (*class* + *-ify* + *-cation*), *hopelessness* (*hope* + *-less* + *-ness*), and *endangerment* (*en-* + *danger* + *-ment*).

Common prefixes include: *anti-, de-, dis-, en-, re-, un-*

Common suffixes include:

- Adjectives: *-able, -al, -ful, -ic, -ing, -ive, -less, -ous, -y*
- Verbs: *-ate, -en, -ify, -ize* (*-ise* in British English)
- Nouns: *-acy, -ance, -cation, -ence, -ity, -ment, -ness, -or, -sion, -tion*

When suffixes are combined, there are often spelling changes. You can use a dictionary to check the correct spelling of these words.

1 **Complete the sentences. Add two or more prefixes or suffixes to the words in parentheses. (The words are all in *Endangered languages*.)**

1 Technology alone is not enough to _____ an endangered language. (vital)

2 The _____ of English is causing other languages to disappear. (popular)

3 Mobile phones are a major cause of the _____ of many languages. (danger)

4 _____ has made the world seem smaller and more closely connected, which has improved life for everyone. (global)

5 Seeing my language used online gives me a feeling of _____. (valid)

6 The _____ of a language depends on children respecting their elders. (vital)

7 The _____ of my language would be a significant loss to the world. (appear)

8 Under ELCat's system of _____, my language would be considered endangered. (class)

2 **Do you agree or disagree with the statements in exercise 1? Discuss them with a partner. Change the sentences so they are true for you.**

RELATIVE PRONOUNS WITH PREPOSITIONS

Academic texts frequently include structures that use relative pronouns with prepositions. These structures include:

- *in which*: This phrase is used as a relative pronoun to describe situations, scenes, and events. (In less formal conversations, people often use *where* instead of *in which*.)

  *...a cultural shift **in which** parents no longer value the language...*

- *some/many/most/all of which, whom*: These are used to describe certain members of a group or category. Use *which* for things and *whom* for people.

  *Communities adopt computers, **most of which** run software in other languages.*

  *Our department has several European employees, **all of whom** speak at least three languages.*

- *of which/whom*: These are usually used before numbers, percentages, amounts, or specific examples.

  *Three hundred and twelve languages were in use, **of which** 123 are now extinct.*

  *The language is spoken by parents, **of whom** very few teach it to their children.*

- Position of prepositions: To avoid ending a sentence in a preposition, some writers place the preposition before *which*. This structure is very formal.

  *ELCat evaluates the situations **in which** it is used.*

  (ELCat evaluates the situations which it is used in.)

  *Which language is usually spoken by the people **with whom** you work?*

  (Which language is usually spoken by the people you work with?)

Complete the paragraph with a preposition + *which* **or** *whom.*

South America is home to hundreds of endangered languages, most (1) _____ are found in the jungles and mountains in the north. This is likely because the places (2) _____ these languages are spoken are extremely remote and not well linked to the outside world. Another long-isolated area of South America is Tierra del Fuego, at the southern tip of the continent. This area is also home to several endangered languages, (3) _____ the best known is probably Yaghan. This language has only one speaker, 84-year-old Cristina Calderón. Since Calderón's sister-in-law died in 2005, she has had no one (4) _____ she can speak her native language. Many people first learned about Yaghan from *Life in a Day*, a documentary film (5) _____ one of the participants talks about Yaghan words. The language has many interesting words, some (6) _____ are quite difficult to define. The word (7) _____ Yaghan is most famous is *mamihlapinatapai*, which has been defined as: the point of time (8) _____ two people want to commence doing something, but neither one wants to be the person to start first.

WRITING Describing changes

You are going to learn about writing definitions of important terms, and you are then going to use this skill to write an essay that describes and analyzes a custom that has become less common.

Writing skill

WRITING DEFINITIONS

Defining key terms is an important part of academic writing, since in many fields of study a term will have a specific meaning that requires a careful and clear explanation. When giving definitions, writers often use the following structures.

- *X refers to / means / is defined as / is a term for Y.*

  "Endangered" **refers to** *a language with between 100 and 1,000 speakers.*

- *Y is called / is referred to as X.*

  A language that has fewer than 1,000 speakers **is called** *an endangered language.*

- *… X, meaning (that) Y.*

  More than 40% of the planet's languages are "endangered," **meaning that** *there are very few living speakers.*

1 Read about six words below. Write sentences defining each word. Use the phrases given.

SIX AMAZING UNTRANSLATABLE WORDS

Word	Definition	Language
1 *pisan zapra*	the length of time needed to eat a banana	Malay
2 *hanyauku*	the act of tiptoeing over warm sand	Kwangali (Namibia)
3 *tartle*	to hesitate while introducing a person because you can't remember his/her name	Scottish (U.K.)
4 *jayus*	a joke that is so unfunny and badly told that a person can't help but laugh	Indonesian
5 *mokita*	something we all know but agree not to talk about	Kilivila (Papua New Guinea)
6 *tingo*	stealing all of your neighbor's possessions by gradually borrowing them one by one	Rapa Nui (Easter Island)

1 refers to   3 is defined as   5 means
2 is called   4 is referred to as   6 is a term for

2 Think of an interesting word in your language or another language. Write a definition for it. Compare words in groups.

An interesting word in Arabic is "gurfa," meaning the amount of water that a person can scoop in one hand.

WRITING TASK

Read the data about two endangered languages. Which language do you think is in greater danger? Write a short essay on the question, giving reasons and supporting your answer with the information.

Audience:	teachers and students
Context:	critical analysis
Purpose:	analyze changes in a culture

Siletz vs. Koro—two endangered languages

LANGUAGE	Siletz (Northwestern U.S.)	Koro (Northeast India)
NUMBER OF NATIVE SPEAKERS	▦ 5 (5,000 in tribe)	▦ 800 (1,200 in tribe)
AGE OF NATIVE SPEAKERS	▦ All elderly	▦ Most older than 20
SPEAKER NUMBER TRENDS	▦ Increasing; younger people learning language	▦ Not clear; researchers first heard of language in 2010
DOMAINS OF USE	▦ Tribal ceremonies ▦ Rarely spoken at home ▦ English is first language for nearly all Siletz people	▦ Used only at home ▦ Not the majority language in any village in the area
REVITALIZATION EFFORTS	▦ Online dictionaries ▦ Classes in local schools and community centers ▦ Tribal government making efforts to save language	▦ Language has not been written down ▦ Researchers working to document language on video and audio now

Siletz in the classroom

(Sources: www.siletzlanguage.org; *New York Times*; *National Geographic*)

BRAINSTORM

As you read the data about the two languages, think about the following:
- Which language has fewer native speakers and young speakers? Which language is losing speakers more quickly?
- Which is used more often in school? Which is more common at home?
- Are people doing enough to keep the language alive?

PLAN

Choose which language you think is in greater danger and think of two or more reasons why you think so. Then create an outline for your essay. Include an introduction, one paragraph for each reason, and a conclusion.

WRITE

Write your essay in around 300 words. Include words with more than one affix and relative pronouns with prepositions. Use the expressions for writing definitions.

SHARE

Exchange essays with a partner. As you read your partner's essay, consider the following points:
- Does the essay say which language is more endangered and give at least two reasons for this view?
- Are important terms in the essay defined?

REWRITE AND EDIT

Consider your partner's comments and rewrite your essay.

STUDY SKILLS Academic referencing

Getting started

Discuss these questions with a partner.

1 What do you understand by these words?

> bibliography   citation   credits   index   reference (list)

Look these words up in a dictionary if you don't know them. How might these words be similar or different?

2 What might be the most important pieces of information you need to supply when giving a source reference?

3 Look at these two references. What information is being given about the sources?

Micelli, F., Myers, J. J. and Murthy, S. S. (2002?). Performance of FRP confined concrete subjected to accelerated environmental conditioning. *In:* Benmokrane, B. and El-Salakawy, E., eds. *Durability of fiber reinforced polymer (FRP) composites for construction: proceedings of the second International Conference (CDCC 02)*, Montreal, May 29–31 2002. Sherbrooke: Université de Sherbrooke, pp. 87–98.

Gadd, E., Oppenheim, C. and Probets, S. (2003). The RoMEO project: protecting metadata in an open access environment. [Online]. (URL http://www.ariadne.ac.uk/issue36/romeo/). *Ariadne,* (36). (Accessed February 12, 2004).

Scenario

Read the scenario and identify Julia's good study skills practices. Why do you think Julia might not be getting top scores in her essays?

Consider it

Do you know that different places of study require different reference styles? Have you heard about these different styles, which provide formats for writing, including how to style references?

MLA—Modern Language Association of America. This style is often used in North America for humanities subjects (except history, which tends to use Chicago Style).

Chicago Style—This refers to the style set out in *The Chicago Manual of Style*.

APA—American Psychological Association of America. (Not to be confused with AP Style—*The Associated Press Stylebook*, for U.S. newspapers.)

Some styles originated with universities, for example **Harvard Style** or **Oxford Style**.

Over to you

Have a look at some bibliographies in the books around you. Do the references look similar to the format in the examples in question 3 above?

These days, writing a bibliography might not be such a hard chore, as software is available to make bibliography writing easier. The next time you need to provide a bibliography, find out what referencing style is expected, as using the wrong style might cost you grades on an otherwise good essay.

Are you aware of what referencing style is needed at your place of study? If not, how can you find out?

Julia is a second-year student, and she transferred to her psychology course from another university after deciding that the engineering program there was not for her.

Julia scored very highly on the psychology midterm exams, but she failed to gain such high grades on her term paper. In her freshman year, Julia scored more highly in her engineering papers than she is doing now.

Julia is competitive about getting the best grades in her class, but no matter how hard she tries, she cannot seem to improve her essay scores. She takes careful notes at every lecture, and she spends countless hours reading through books and websites at the library. She creates detailed summaries of all the information she finds in these books and effectively paraphrases in order to avoid plagiarism. She is also aware of the importance of listing her sources, and she lists source references exactly as she used to do in her engineering essays at her old university.

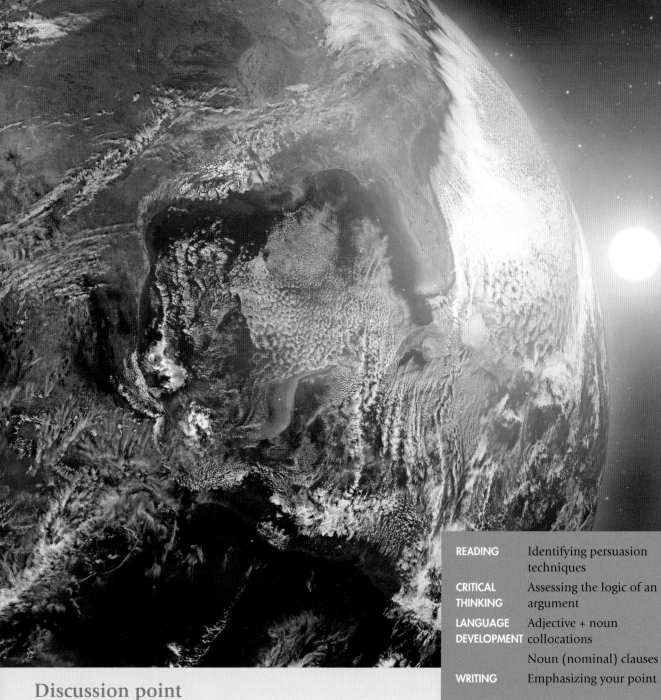

Expanse

READING	Identifying persuasion techniques
CRITICAL THINKING	Assessing the logic of an argument
LANGUAGE DEVELOPMENT	Adjective + noun collocations
	Noun (nominal) clauses
WRITING	Emphasizing your point

Discussion point

Discuss these questions with a partner.

1 What is the approximate population of our planet? Does the figure concern you? Why or why not?

2 Look at the global issues below. Which do you think are the most serious? Rank them from 1 (least serious) to 6 (most serious).

> crime   debt   global warming   nuclear weapons   population size   poverty

3 Compare your ranking to a partner's. Which do you both agree are the two biggest issues that need to be addressed? Why?

Vocabulary preview

What do you think the underlined words mean? Discuss your ideas with a partner.

a   Natural fresh water is ¹scarce in the United Arab Emirates.

b   India's large population is ²putting a strain on natural resources.

c   Germany is interested in ³tapping into ⁴renewable energy sources, such as wind and solar power, to create more ⁵sustainable living.

d   New Orleans is suffering from ⁶urban sprawl as the city grows.

e   Ancient Egyptians used flood water from the Nile to ⁷irrigate their farmland.

f   The people of Easter Island ⁸died out because of deforestation and ⁹soil erosion, which stopped them from growing anything.

g   One of the most ¹⁰thriving areas for ¹¹biodiversity is the Great Barrier Reef in Australia.

h   The ¹²worst case scenario for the future of our planet is a continued increase in world population.

READING   Overpopulation: A problem or a myth? 🇺🇸 🇬🇧

Before you read

Work with a partner. What benefits and problems does a growing population bring to a country and to the world?

Global reading

1   **Read the article *Overpopulation: A problem or a myth?* on pages 70–71. What reasons do the writers give to support their arguments that overpopulation is a problem or a myth?**

> ### IDENTIFYING PERSUASION TECHNIQUES
>
> Writers of texts that include arguments may use techniques to try to persuade the reader to agree with them. As well as putting forward a logical argument, persuasion techniques include the following:
>
> * Repeating or paraphrasing arguments to emphasize them.
>
>   *… an extra 2 billion people—the same number of people who currently live in the African and American continents combined.*
>
> * The inclusion of insights into the future to show the reader the consequences of an action.
>
>   *It is likely that demand for oil over the next fifty years will push prices up further.*
>
> * The dismissal of alternative arguments by providing different evidence or by examining evidence from a different perspective.
>
>   *… the size of families is actually decreasing.*
>
> Writers of more informal texts such as newspapers/blogs may include the following:
>
> * The use of questions to involve the reader.
>
>   *Who can argue with free and equal education for everyone?*
>
> * The use of vocabulary related to feelings to engage the reader emotionally.
>
>   *We must stop burying our heads in the sand.*

2   **Read Marilyn Cratchley's article again and find one example of each of the techniques in the box.**

3   **Whose argument did you find most persuasive? Why?**

Critical thinking skill

1 **Look at these numbers from Dr. Rice's article. Do they describe a trend (a gradual change or development), a pattern (a series of repeated actions or events, cf. p. 49) or a static figure?**

   a 2bn   **b** 2.5%   **c** one in three   **d** 10%   **e** 1.5bn   **f** 20m

2 **What point is Dr. Rice making with each trend/pattern?**

ASSESSING THE LOGIC OF AN ARGUMENT

After identifying arguments in an academic text, it is necessary to assess the logic of each argument to ensure it is valid. Consider this example argument:

All people are materialistic. Materialism is bad, as research shows it harms the environment. Therefore, all people are bad.

To test the logic of an argument, you can:

- Consider whether the statement on which the argument is based is true. Is it a generalization (a statement that is true in most situations, but not all)? Is it an assumption (something you consider likely to be true but you have no proof)? Or is it speculation (something which is possible)? If so, are these reasonable? You might need to conduct research, such as referring to the Internet, to find out.

  All people are materialistic. (= unreasonable generalization)

  Some people are materialistic. (= reasonable assumption, or speculation)

- Examine the evidence that supports the argument. Is it sufficient? Is it current, reliable, valid, and relevant?

  Research shows materialism harms the environment. (What research? How does it harm the environment? This is insufficient.)

- Consider: Do all the points follow logically from one another?

  Therefore, all people are bad. (Shouldn't the logical conclusion be that people harm the environment rather than that they are bad?)

---

3 **Read *Overpopulation: A problem or a myth?* again. Analyze the arguments below. Are they logical? Is there enough evidence to support them?**

A problem
1 An increase in demand for clean drinking water will result in more disease.
2 Farmers will risk using more waste water if fresh water becomes scarcer.
3 Deforestation and mining affect our ecosystem and the biodiversity within it.
4 The number of cars on our roads is increasing.
5 Education is the solution to overpopulation.

A myth
6 The amount of fresh water has not changed in 10,000 years.
7 Materialism and overconsumption are facts of life for everyone in the western world.
8 Waste is a common occurrence.
9 Developing countries will generate greater wealth in future.
10 People will change consumption habits if they are educated.

4 **Which writer presented the better and more logical arguments? Why?**

Developing critical thinking

Discuss these questions in a group.

1 How do you think education helps to reduce the size of families?
2 How do you think the problem of overconsumption can be addressed? What can these people do: individuals, schools, governments, business leaders? Think of at least one action point for each group.

OVERPOPULATION:
A problem or a myth?

Argument A:

A problem 🇺🇸
By ecologist Dr. Alexander J. Rice

[1] In 2011, the population of the world reached 7 billion people. The UN Population Division (2009) predicts the number could be as high as 9 billion by 2050; that is an increase of 2 billion people—the same number of people who currently live in the African and American continents combined—living on Earth, using its resources to survive.

[2] Although families are getting smaller, people are living longer because medical and technical advances have meant that the effect of infectious diseases has been reduced. As a result the UN's worst case scenario for 2100 is that the world population will reach almost 16 billion (UN, 2011). That is more than twice the number of people we have today. And yet already we are placing enormous pressure on the Earth. The kind of pressure that, if increased, could have a profound and irreversible effect on our planet.

[3] The first major issue is water. Just 2.5% of the world's water is fresh, with much of that caught up in polar ice caps (University of Michigan, 2000). Drought and poor infrastructure mean that already today water is a scarce resource. Over 1 billion people lack access to clean water and one in three people in every continent does not have enough water to satisfy their daily needs (WHO, 2009). Without clean drinking water, there will be a rapid rise in diseases such as cholera and typhoid, which will place a greater strain on healthcare systems. Without water for agriculture and industry, our food and manufacturing industries will be unable to meet demand. Already today, 10% of people consume foods which have been irrigated using waste water full of chemicals or disease (WHO, 2009). This is likely to increase if water becomes even scarcer.

[4] The second major issue is land. Current agricultural practices and the impact of pollution both contribute to soil erosion and a decreased level of soil fertility. It is estimated that 1.5 billion people depend on land which is degraded (FAO, 2008). Deforestation and mining have a huge impact on our ecosystem and the biodiversity on which it thrives. The WWF (n.d.) estimates that we may be losing ten thousand species every year. All of this affects the number of crops that can be grown and creates greater food insecurity. How can we allow this destruction to occur under our noses when we know that our land is already degraded?

[5] Another prime concern is energy. Governments, such as those in the U.S. and Germany, are starting to invest in renewable energy to reduce their reliance on oil and tap into resources with greater sustainability. However, the number of road vehicles reached a billion in 2010 (WardsAuto, 2011), an increase of 20 million from the previous year, and is continuing to increase. It is therefore likely that there will be a higher demand for oil over the next fifty years, which will push prices higher. This will make it more difficult for people to afford food, heating, and other manufactured goods, placing more people into poverty.

[6] Overpopulation is not a problem for one country or continent; it is a problem for all of us. The UN (2012) estimates that by 2030 the world will need 50% more food, 30% more water, and 45% more energy than it does today. We must stop burying our heads in the sand and make a bigger effort to reduce population growth, which means increasing access to education. Large families tend to be prevalent in developing countries and yet when men, women, and children in these areas receive education, family sizes are reduced. The UN estimates that in less developed countries where women are not educated, they have twice as many children as those countries where they are educated. It is therefore this area in which we should invest time and money. Who can argue with free and equal education for everyone?

Argument B:
A myth 🇬🇧
By environmentalist Marilyn Cratchley

[1] It is true that world population is growing, but this is not the cause of our current and future global problems. Believing this will cause us to ignore the real problem and risk long-term damage to our planet.

[2] Let me start by explaining why overpopulation is a myth. The UN Population Division regularly predicts population growth but provides a low variant, medium variant, and high variant to factor in various possibilities. In the 2010 revision, their high variant suggests that the world population will be almost 16 billion in 2100, but the low variant predicts it will peak at 8 billion and decrease to just over 6 billion by 2100. In most cases, it is the low variant that has come true in the past (*Overpopulation Is a Myth. com*, Episode 1, Population Research Institute. Web. 10 Jun. 2013), suggesting the same will be true of their future population predictions. In addition to this, the size of families is actually decreasing. The average woman now has 2.5 children, which is very close to the replacement level of 2.3 (World Bank, 2009), and in many countries the fertility rate is even lower.

[3] For the Earth to be overpopulated, there needs to be insufficient food, water, and space for humans to live. Indian economist Raj Krishna estimates that India alone is capable of increasing crop yields to the point of providing the entire world's food supply. The World Food Programme (n.d.) confirms that there is sufficient food grown to feed the world and there is the same amount of fresh water on the planet now as there was 10,000 years ago; it has simply been redistributed. So how is it possible that the number of people in the world is impacting on our planet?

[4] It is not an increase in population that is a severe threat. It is an increase in consumption. Materialism and overconsumption are facts of life for everybody in the western world, as possessions reflect a person's status in society and people strive to obtain happiness through owning the latest fashionable goods. Not only that, but waste is a common occurrence which has a huge impact on our resources. In addition, our current consumption is imbalanced, unsustainable, and estimated to be 30% more than the Earth can regenerate (LaTouche, n.d.). It is a sad truth that 80% of the world's resources are currently used by just 20% of the world's population (UN, 2008), which means that a fifth of us use four-fifths of the world's food and energy.

[5] Our overconsumption must be addressed now to make our lives more sustainable and avoid continuing the horrendous damage to the environment we are causing. With more developing countries set to generate greater wealth, there is bound to be a substantial increase in overconsumption in the future, so we must be prepared today. The key is education. The more people understand about the consequences of their materialism, the fewer resources they are likely to consume. Attitudes must be changed if our consumption habits are to change. If we do not work towards this, but instead focus on the wrong issue, we may find ourselves living on a planet that can no longer sustain human life.

ACADEMIC KEYWORDS		
insufficient	(adj)	/ˌɪnsəˈfɪʃ(ə)nt/
profound	(adj)	/prəˈfaʊnd/
substantial	(adj)	/səbˈstænʃ(ə)l/

Language development

ADJECTIVE + NOUN COLLOCATIONS

Adjectives that are synonyms often do not collocate with the same noun.
There's a **large number** of people in the world.
~~There's a **big number** of people in the world.~~
This has a **serious effect** on our planet.
~~This has a **strong effect** on our planet.~~

1 Choose the appropriate adjective to collocate with the noun to complete the sentences from the article *Overpopulation: A problem or a myth?*

1 Already we are placing **enormous / large** pressure on the Earth.

2 It could have a **prime / profound** and irreversible effect on our planet.

3 The first **major / substantial** issue is water.

4 There will be a **fast / rapid** rise in diseases.

5 This will place a **greater / higher** strain on healthcare systems.

6 Another **prime / severe** concern is energy.

7 Deforestation and mining have a **high / huge** impact on our ecosystem.

8 Governments are starting to tap into resources with **bigger / greater** sustainability.

9 It is therefore likely that there will be a **higher / more severe** demand for oil, which will push prices higher.

10 We must make a **bigger / higher** effort to reduce population growth.

2 Complete each sentence with the appropriate adjective.

1   considerable   systematic   widespread

    a Education is of _____ importance in fighting overpopulation.

    b There is a _____ but incorrect belief that overpopulation is a developing world problem.

    c We must take a _____ approach to the overpopulation problem.

2   crucial   prominent   substantial

    a A _____ number of people are unaware of problems caused by overconsumption.

    b A _____ factor in overconsumption is our desire to own material goods.

    c The UN Population Division is the _____ expert in population growth.

3   acute   leading   principal

    a One of the _____ aims of the UN Population Division is to monitor population growth.

    b Overconsumption will create _____ shortages in resources.

    c Our increasing demand for goods is one of the _____ causes of environmental destruction.

3 Think about three issues that people in your country are concerned about—e.g., pollution, water shortages, traffic congestion, unemployment, immigration. Make some sentences about them using six of the adjective + noun collocations in exercises 1 and 2.

NOUN (NOMINAL) CLAUSES

A noun (nominal) clause is a group of words that performs the same function as a noun. The noun clause can be the subject or object of a sentence.

Families are getting smaller. (noun as subject)

How we deal with this situation is actually quite simple. (noun clause as subject)

The first major issue is water. (noun as object)

The UN estimates that by 2030 the world will need 50% more food. (noun clause as object)

Noun clauses include clauses which follow *that*, *if/whether*, and questions.

- *That* clauses usually come after adjectives or verbs describing thoughts and opinions, and reporting verbs (e.g., *notice, estimate, suggest*). The word *that* can be omitted.

  People are concerned that oil prices are rising.

  It is believed we will need 50% more food in future.

- Question clauses include question words such as *how, what, when*. They answer the question.

  Pollution is what worries me the most. (*What worries you the most?*)

- We use *if/whether* to place *yes/no* questions in a statement.

  We must ask ourselves whether we can really cope. (*Can we cope?*)

  We have no idea if we are damaging the planet beyond repair. (*Are we damaging the planet beyond repair?*)

1 Underline the noun clauses in the sentences below.

1 People today know they can follow fashion without spending much.
2 People do not always realize that fast fashion affects the environment.
3 People may not be aware that polyester is made from petroleum.
4 What may result from this is the release of harmful gases.
5 How cotton is grown varies, but pesticides may be used.
6 People should think carefully about whether they need new clothes or not.

2 Complete the noun phrases in italics in the sentences with an appropriate word(s). There may be more than one possibility.

1 It is clear _____ *we have become a throw-away society.*
2 I don't think _____ *many people fix things that break anymore.*
3 _____ *authorities dispose of unwanted goods* is becoming a huge problem.
4 It is sad _____ *most things we buy only last a couple of years.*
5 _____ *most companies do these days is make products that don't last.*
6 Perhaps we should question _____ *we need so much packaging when we buy things.*

3 Work with a partner and discuss whether you agree with the statements in exercise 2. Discuss why or why not.

WRITING A persuasive essay

You are going to learn about different techniques you can use to emphasize your point when you are presenting an idea or an argument. You are then going to write a persuasive essay on the topic of education.

Writing skill

EMPHASIZING YOUR POINT

A writer might emphasize a point of view. This can be done in the following ways:

*   Sentences starting with preparatory *It*

    The biggest companies should be concerned. / ***It is the biggest companies*** *that should be concerned.*

*   *What* noun clauses

    We need to work together. / ***What we need is*** *to work together.*

*   Inversion of the subject and negative adverb

    A solution is seldom discussed. / ***Seldom is*** *a solution discussed.*

1 Complete the second sentence so it means the same as the first.

1 World population began to increase more quickly only when humans started to grow crops and keep farm animals.
   Only when …

2 Many people do not realize that our world cannot continue to sustain our needs.
   What many people …

3 World leaders rarely discuss the issue of overpopulation.
   Rarely …

4 Governments should address the issue of world poverty.
   It is …

5 Education helps people escape poverty and understand global issues.
   Not only …

6 Men are more likely to be educated than women.
   It is men …

7 We should address these issues now and not in the future.
   It is now that …

2 Work with a partner. Why is literacy important?

3 Read the article below. Does it include your ideas?

4 Rewrite the underlined parts of the article using the words/expressions in the box to add emphasis.

> does   it is…   not only…   rarely   what you have…

Literacy: a vital skill

The impact of education on a person is enormous, but ¹the ability to read and write affects your life the most. ²You don't often find work without it that allows you to advance economically and become socially mobile. Although illiteracy does not stop you living your life, ³it makes you feel isolated from the wider society and brings about a sense of loneliness. ⁴You have to rely on other people, and as a result, you may be less independent with regard to the decisions you make. ⁵Illiteracy affects a person individually and reduces the level of economic development a country experiences.

WRITING TASK

You are going to write a persuasive essay on behalf of an international charity giving reasons why education for all children is necessary in the fight against overpopulation.

Read the introduction to an academic essay on the benefits of education for children. Look at the underlined items. Are they examples of persuasive techniques (*P*), adjective + noun collocations (*A*), or emphasis (*E*)?

Audience:	a teacher and students
Context:	a persuasive essay
Purpose:	prioritize, emphasize, and persuade

[1]Can you imagine a world where education is free for all children? It is a world where young people grow up into adults who have a [2]great understanding of the world they live in, improving their health and allowing them to better themselves and their economic situation. This means [3]not only more money for themselves but also for their countries through [4]higher taxation and [5]greater economic stability. It is possible that a world like this can exist through the commitment of people in power and educational organizations around the world. In this essay, I will argue that education is a [6]basic human right that should be free for all children.

BRAINSTORM

How can education for all children help to overcome overpopulation? Complete the notes with your ideas.

General—70 million children do not attend school. Millions start but do not finish (World Bank, 2012). Why? Effects?

Health—Cutler & Lleras-Muney (2006) research, education improves health. How? Effects?

Poverty—UNESCO (2006), the higher the number of school years, the higher GDP per capita of the country. Why? Effects?

PLAN

Plan your essay. Use your ideas above and organize them into the paragraph plan below.

Introduction: _____

Reason 1: _____

Reason 2: _____

Reason 3: _____

Conclusion: _____

WRITE

Write your essay in around 300 words. Use appropriate persuasion techniques. Emphasize key information, and include some adjective + noun collocations and some different noun clauses. These will add variety and complexity to your writing.

SHARE

Exchange your essay with a partner. Read the checklist below and give feedback to your partner.
- Is the essay well organized?
- Is the essay persuasive?
- Has your partner emphasized any information?
- Has your partner included adjective + noun collocations?

REWRITE AND EDIT

Consider your partner's comments and rewrite your essay.

Argument: Persuasion through reasons

by Stella Cottrell

Persuasion and reasons

In everyday language, an 'argument' can suggest poor communication, a difficult relationship, hard feelings, and, possibly, aggression. This is not the case with argument as part of critical thinking. An 'argument' merely means presenting reasons to support your position or point of view. If other people accept those reasons, they are more likely to be persuaded to your point of view.

An argument includes:

- a position or point of view;
- an attempt to persuade others to accept that point of view;
- reasons given to support the point of view.

To identify an argument, it is useful to keep in mind such questions as:

- 'What was the point of producing this text or programme?'
- 'What is the main message I am supposed to take from this?'
- 'What does the author/producer want me to believe, accept or do?'
- 'What reasons have they offered to support their position?'

In most circumstances, authors aim to persuade us to a particular point of view because they believe in what they are saying. However, in some cases, they may have an obvious or a hidden vested interest. It may be that they have a long-standing rivalry with academics from a different school of thought. It may be that they work for a company that wants their audience to buy its products or to subscribe to a particular view on health or pollution or genetics.

Authors may also intentionally, or unintentionally, interpret information through the filter of their own political, religious or ideological perspectives. That doesn't necessarily make their argument invalid, but it is often important to know their theoretical position in order to identify the influences on their line of reasoning.

Ambiguous arguments

Sometimes, for everyday purposes, a statement may be clear and uncontroversial. For example:

'It's raining'—when clearly it is raining.

'Everyone who ate the fish is ill'—when this is an observation of fact.

'I ran a mile in 4 minutes'—when this has been timed and observed.

More often, there are complexities in what we hear, see, and read. It may not be obvious what point someone is trying to make, or we may suspect that there are half-truths in what they say. We recognise this in speech when we make comments such as 'What's your point?' or 'What are you trying to say?' We may wonder how someone has arrived at a particular conclusion: what they say just doesn't seem to 'add up'. When this is obvious, we may be able to point it out and resolve the misunderstanding.

However, when we are reading books or watching television, the author isn't available to answer queries about what is meant. The argument may be very complicated and it can take time to clarify the line of reasoning through careful analysis and close reading or observation. The author may also have presented the information in such a way that the lack of evidence, the illogical arguments or false conclusions are not immediately apparent. Critical thinking skills are then particularly important because we cannot always ask directly for explanations and clarifications.

Change

READING	Identifying concepts and theories
CRITICAL THINKING	Inferring criticism
LANGUAGE DEVELOPMENT	Idiomatic language
	Participle clauses
WRITING	Report writing

Discussion point

Discuss these questions with a partner.

1 How has the product in this picture changed in the last hundred years?
2 Why do companies regularly change their products and systems?
3 What happens if a company doesn't change its products or systems?

Vocabulary preview

1 Work with a partner. Decide if the statements about the words in italics are true (T) or false (F).

1 A *business model* is a manager who works for a fashion company. ___

2 The *peak* of a mountain is the top part. ___

3 If you *drive a company forward*, you cause it to be unsuccessful. ___

4 If you *empower* someone, you take their power away. ___

5 *Creating a vision* describes the business process of building a public image. ___

6 Companies try to *incentivize* their staff by giving them a financial reason to work hard. ___

7 A *mentoring scheme* involves less experienced people helping more experienced people. ___

8 If you *execute* a strategy, you stop it. ___

2 Correct the sentences which are false. Do not change the words in italics.

READING Leadership and change management 🇬🇧

Before you read

Work with a partner and make a list of five successful companies that you know. What has made them successful? How have they changed over the years?

Global reading

> **■ IDENTIFYING CONCEPTS AND THEORIES ■**
>
> Some texts present concepts or theories rather than arguments. A concept is a general idea about something that exists or an idea about how something should be done. An argument is a point of view.
>
> *Lewin's change model includes a three-step approach to change management known as Unfreeze, Change, Refreeze. (= a concept/theory)*
>
> *People do not always like change. In a 2013 survey, 76% of company workers said they wanted their circumstances to stay the same. It is therefore important for companies to implement change carefully. (= an argument)*
>
> You may come across several different concepts on the same theme. You might need to compare concepts in order to decide which is most compelling.

1 You are going to read an excerpt from a business studies textbook by Janelle Franklin entitled *Leadership and change management* on pages 80–81. First, look at the three headings. Each one represents a business model related to change management. Match each model to its description.

a A detailed, step-by-step approach to managing change

b A theory of how change affects individuals within an organization

c A simple three-step approach to change management

2 Read *Leadership and change management* and decide if the statements below are true (T) or false (F).

1 Companies should spend time celebrating their successes.

2 Lewin's model remains influential today.

3 Three-quarters of change management strategies are successful.

4 According to Fisher, all employees experience the same emotions when experiencing change at work.

3 Read *Leadership and change management* a second time and decide whether the features belong to Lewin's model (*L*), Kotter's model (*K*), or Fisher's model (*F*). Some features exist in more than one model.

1 It starts by raising employees' awareness that change is important.
2 It motivates staff to want to be part of the change.
3 It connects employees with experienced members of staff who can support them.
4 It puts people and their experiences at the heart of the model.
5 It empowers staff.
6 It is based on the idea that emotions need to be managed.
7 A group of people are chosen to lead the change strategy.
8 The final stages involve the changes being accepted.

4 Draw a Venn diagram of the three models and place the features (1–8) in exercise 3 into the appropriate place. Which two models have the most in common?

5 Read the excerpt again. What analogies does the writer use to describe the following?

1 How some well-known companies have been too slow to innovate

Admiring the view too long on a mountain without realizing there is more to climb.

2 The task of creating and implementing a change management strategy
3 Lewin's Unfreeze, Change, Refreeze model
4 People's individual experiences of change

Critical thinking skill

INFERRING CRITICISM

Although most academic writing strives for balance and impartiality, some authors may criticise an idea or argument that they are discussing without specifically saying they dislike it. Be aware of your own and/or an author's personal opinions on a topic, which may not be objective. For example, in the excerpt below, the underlined words suggest the author is critical of businesses that do not try to keep up with a changing market.

The need for change is <u>obvious</u> and <u>yet</u> businesses around the world <u>fail</u> to actively work towards change, <u>unnecessarily</u> <u>suffering</u> the <u>consequences</u> as a result.

1 Read the first paragraph of the excerpt again and underline the sentence which shows criticism. Which words help you?

2 Check the things below that the writer is critical of. Why?

1 ☐ The behavior of Apple®, Google, and Amazon (para. 1)
2 ☐ The behavior of other companies (para. 1)
3 ☐ Companies whose change management strategies fail (para. 2)
4 ☐ Lewin's Unfreeze, Change, Refreeze model (para. 3)
5 ☐ Kotter's eight-step model (para. 7)
6 ☐ John M. Fisher's model of personal change (para. 9)

Developing critical thinking

Discuss these questions in a group.

1 Which of the three change models in the excerpt do you think would be most useful to a company preparing for change? Why?
2 Think about Fisher's model of personal change. What should the senior managers of a company do to reduce negative feelings experienced by staff during a period of change?
3 What do you think senior managers of a company should do to incentivize staff to work hard?

Leadership & Change Management

Janelle Franklin

1 Like a climber reaching a mountain peak, leading businesses must not spend too long standing and admiring the view or they may find themselves swiftly overtaken by leaner and more adaptable mountaineers. Successful companies such as Apple, Google, and Amazon are all examples of industry leaders which understand that they still have a mountain to climb; while other companies have mistakenly spent far too long looking at the scenery, not appreciating that further heights were there to be scaled.

2 We are all aware that if a business wants to succeed, it has to create a culture of innovation in a fast-changing market. When one company innovates, others will quickly follow suit. Without continued creativity, a business will become stagnant, lose its competitive edge and very quickly find itself behind the times. The need for change is obvious and yet businesses around the world fail to actively work towards change, unnecessarily suffering the consequences. Company bosses making a commitment to change is the first, and easy, step forward. However, planning and executing a change strategy can be an uphill struggle, with organisations often pulling the plug on strategies at the first sign of difficulty. Fortunately, there is a lot of support for businesses in the academic field of change management, with several business models to draw on.

Lewin's Unfreeze, Change, Refreeze model

3 The need to manage change first came to prominence with a three-stage theory by Kurt Lewin (1947) known as Unfreeze, Change, Refreeze. As a physicist and social psychologist, Lewin uses a block of ice to explain his theory. He suggests that if you have a square block of ice but you want a cone-shaped block of ice, you need to melt it (unfreeze), change it into a cone-shape (change), and then solidify the new shape (refreeze). He suggests a three-stage approach:

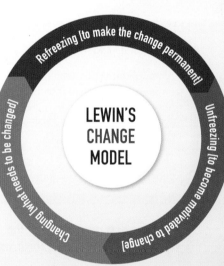

* People become aware that change is necessary and prepare themselves for it.

* A mentoring scheme is implemented to support employees who are given the power to find their own solutions to problems.

* The change becomes normal behaviour for the organisation.

It is the final stage which companies may struggle to apply in today's fast-moving world; a place where there is little time for stability. However, this model has been, and continues to be, highly influential in the business world and its impact is noticeable in more recent models.

Kotter's eight-step approach to change management

4 One of the more recent models of change was created by Dr John Kotter (1995) and is an eight-step approach to change management, a more robust template for change that business leaders can follow to build a detailed plan. Having spent thirty years researching change management strategies in companies, Kotter realised that 70% of them fail and so created this model as a way of helping those businesses to avoid that problem.

5 Kotter's first step involves creating a sense of urgency. Like Lewin's Unfreeze stage, it focuses on explaining to people why change is necessary to drive the company forward, creating a buzz around the company that inspires people to participate. The next three stages involve the putting in place of leaders and other key people who have the expertise and respect to push change forward. They create a vision which is simple and motivating and then communicate it to everyone in the organisation, encouraging two-way communication in the process.

KOTTER'S EIGHT-STEP APPROACH TO CHANGE MANAGEMENT

Step 8: Incorporating changes into the culture
Step 7: Never letting up
Step 6: Generating short-term wins
Step 5: Empowering broad-based action
Step 4: Communicating the vision
Step 3: Developing a change vision
Step 2: Guiding the leading coalition
Step 1: Creating sense of urgency

[6] Steps five to seven involve empowering staff through skills development and new systems of work before setting short-term goals that people can achieve. By pushing forward and not giving up, the company can show staff that the changes are producing small, but successful results. In the end, in step eight, the changes become accepted as part of the company culture.

Fisher's model of personal change

[7] Kotter's model is very much a top-down process, where leaders at the top drive the changes. Yet one of the biggest reasons for the high failure rate of change management strategies is the people involved. It is easy for a change management strategy to focus solely on systems, but it is in fact people who pose the greatest threat to its success. By dealing with people appropriately, the strategy has a much greater chance of survival. For this reason, John M Fisher (2005) created a model of personal change to examine an individual's experiences of change in an organisation. He likens it to crossing from one peak to another, suggesting that an individual will go through a series of emotions during the crossing. These are: anxiety, happiness, fear, threat, guilt, depression, gradual acceptance, and moving forward. How exactly a person experiences these emotions depends very much on how the change was instigated, how much control that individual has, their self-image, and past experiences of change, meaning that each person's journey is different.

[8] Imagine that an accounting manager has been asked to implement new accounts systems to modernise the department. Fisher suggests that the manager will start with a feeling of *anxiety* caused by a lack of understanding about the changes; he will be concerned about how they will affect him and whether he can cope with them. The manager will then feel *happy* because things are finally going to change, but when he realises that he will have to change his behaviour, he will start to feel *fear*. The next stage is *threat*, as the manager starts to self-reflect about his behaviour and actions at work and begins to perceive himself differently. It may become apparent, for example, that he is less able to adapt to new computer software than he expected and finds members of his team are more competent than he is. This leads to *guilt* and may result in *depression* as he loses a sense of who he is. Eventually, having found his feet within the new environment and becoming more skilled at using the software, there will be *gradual acceptance*. Finally, he will feel as if he can *move forward*.

[9] Fisher's model provides businesses with a comprehensive and solid understanding of how much of an impact change may have on employees across the board. This understanding can be fed into a strategic plan ensuring that these feelings are managed appropriately. He goes on further to suggest ways in which this can be done.

Fisher's model of personal change

anxiety / happiness / fear / threat / guilt / depression / gradual acceptance / moving forward

ACADEMIC KEYWORDS

apply	(v)	/əˈplaɪ/
commitment	(n)	/kəˈmɪtmənt/
competitive	(adj)	/kəmˈpetətɪv/

Language development

IDIOMATIC LANGUAGE

Most academic texts avoid idioms, preferring to use formal, literal language which is precise in its meaning. However, you may come across some idiomatic language when reading more informal texts, such as newspaper or magazine articles, and books on less academic subjects.

*What comes next, however, can be **an uphill struggle** (= a very difficult thing to do), with organizations often **pulling the plug** (= stopping/quitting) on strategies at the first sign of difficulty.*

1 **Find the idioms 1–5 in *Leadership and change management* and match them to the definitions a–e.**

1	mountain to climb (para. 1)	a	make a strong feeling of excitement
2	follow suit (para. 2)	b	a difficult task to reach a goal
3	behind the times (para. 2)	c	involving everyone
4	create a buzz (para. 5)	d	do what someone else is doing
5	across the board (para. 9)	e	not modern or making as much progress as others

2 **Look at the underlined idioms in the blog comment below. What do you think they mean?**

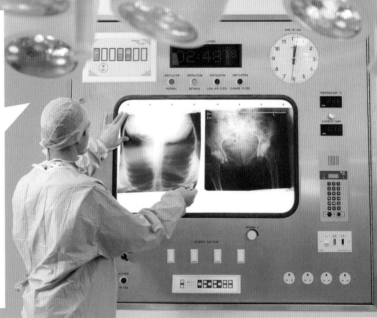

I ¹beg to differ with the views of Dr. Porter and suggest he has been too quick to ²leap to the wrong conclusions. ³State-of-the-art technology is ⁴by no means the only way in which a company can be competitive. In fact, ⁵the bottom line is that the biggest asset of most organizations is their people and without them being innovative and ⁶moving with the times, a company will suffer. If companies follow Dr. Porter's advice and invest all their time and energy in technology without getting their staff ⁷on board with the changes, then their attempts to have a competitive edge will ⁸fall at the first hurdle. Of course technology is important, but it is just ⁹the tip of the iceberg in what is a complex issue. An issue that is obviously not as ¹⁰clear-cut as Dr. Porter suggests.

3 **Choose the correct bold word in these definitions of the idioms in exercise 2.**

1 disagree **politely** / **strongly**
2 take a view on something when **knowing** / **not knowing** all the facts
3 **least** / **most** advanced
4 **definitely** / **possibly** not
5 the most **basic** / **difficult** fact or issue
6 adapting your behavior because the world **changes** / **stands still**
7 **motivated by** / **supporting**
8 **fail** / **succeed** at the beginning
9 a small indication of a problem that shows a **less** / **more** serious situation exists
10 **difficult** / **easy** to understand

PARTICIPLE CLAUSES

Participle clauses are common in formal writing. The present participle (-ing) has an active meaning. The past participle (-ed) has a passive meaning.

- We use participle clauses to express cause, effect, and condition.

   Having spent thirty years researching change management systems in companies, he realized that 70% of them fail. (= Because he had spent)

   Businesses fail to change, **suffering** the consequences. (= as a result, they suffer)

   Introduced effectively, schemes can be successful. (= If they are introduced)

- We can use participle clauses to describe time with on, while, after, before.

   On/While facing reduced sales, the company implemented change. (= When they were facing)

   Before creating a strategy, the company employed a strategist. (= Before they created)

   After experiencing a period of change, the staff wanted stability. (= After they experienced)

- We use the perfect participle (having + -ed verb) when we want to say that an action finished before another action.

   Eventually, **having found** his feet within the new environment, there will be gradual acceptance. (= because he has found his feet)

1 Rewrite the sentences using a participle clause. Use the prompts to help you.

1 Because they wanted to create a change strategy, senior managers brought in a consultant.
   Wanting …

2 When they were reading the consultant's report, they realized they needed to organize a meeting.
   While …

3 The meeting took place in the boardroom and was attended by all management.
   Attended …

4 When they heard about the report, the managers had a lot of questions.
   On …

2 Rewrite the sentences, replacing the underlined section with a participle clause.

1 <u>As some staff members heard about the changes</u>, they became angry.

2 Some staff members resigned <u>because they wanted things to stay the same</u>.

3 <u>After they explained the need for change</u>, managers received positive feedback from the staff.

4 <u>All staff received training</u> and successfully coped with the changes.

3 Complete the sentences about you, your family, friends, etc.

1 On starting this course …

2 Having heard the good news about …,

3 Being a student, …

4 After seeing …,

5 Having visited …,

6 While watching …,

WRITING Report writing

You are going to learn how to write a report and punctuate the text within a report appropriately. You are then going to use this information to write a report using the correct structure and punctuation.

Writing skill

▌REPORT WRITING ▌

In business, science, and technical courses you may be required to write a report. A good report is clear, concise, and divided into sections which will always include an introduction, a main body, and a conclusion. Each section will have a heading.

A report may also include:

- An abstract/executive summary (the essential elements of the report);
- Method and materials (related to an experiment);
- Recommendations (things that arise from your conclusions);
- A bibliography (references you source in your report); and
- Appendices (information that is too big to go in the main body).

Report writers sometimes use bullet points as above to present information simply.

1 **The report below has been written by the HR director of a small company. Read it and decide where the headings in the box should be placed.**

> Conclusions   Introduction   Recommendations
> Research method   Results

Buckson's supermarket

Buckson's is a local grocery store located in a large residential area of the town. It first opened in 1924 and has been a family business ever since. Because sales have been dropping slowly for the last ten years, research has been conducted to find out the reasons why. The research involved face-to-face interviews with thirty Buckson's customers and thirty customers of the closest rival supermarket, Shop Mart. The interviews lasted approximately ten minutes and included fifteen questions. The results of the research established that customers are purchasing fewer items due to long lines at the check-out, no Internet presence, and no delivery service. The results also showed that customers believe Buckson's goods to be of high quality. Bakery goods are freshly made. Several customers said, "They make the best cakes in town." They think the staff are friendlier and more helpful than those at the nearest competitor. Overall analysis of the results suggests that customers would be happy to pay Buckson's prices if they were able to receive faster check-out service and were given the opportunity to order food online or in the store which is later delivered. It is highly recommended that Buckson's invest in a higher speed Internet connection and faster scanners to avoid long lines at the check-out, create an online shopping facility including a shopping app that can be downloaded onto mobile phones, and purchase vans in which food can be delivered. In addition, a strategy should be put in place to ensure that current staff members are able to adapt to the new changes, and continue to provide a high-quality service to customers.

2 **Decide how some parts of the report should be changed to make it clearer and more concise. Think also about bullet points and punctuation, for example:**

The research involved:
- face-to-face interviews with 30 Buckson's customers
- face-to-face interviews with 30 Shop Mart customers

WRITING TASK

Read the report introduction. What is the purpose of the report?

Introduction

Buckson's supermarket has committed to modernizing its operations over the next twelve months by investing in:

- a new, faster check-out system
- a new website and app
- a van delivery service.

Having worked at the company for over ten years, 50% of the staff are very much used to the traditional approach of the company. There is a concern that some of these staff will struggle with the changes, resulting in the strategic aims of the company not being met (i.e., increased profits). As a result, Buckson's would like to implement a program that ensures all staff are able to work within the new system. The purpose of this report, written by TWC Management Consultancy, is to make recommendations as to what that program should involve.

Imagine you work for TWC Management Consultancy. Write the rest of the report, giving practical suggestions on how Buckson's supermarket can ensure that all staff are prepared and support the forthcoming company changes.

BRAINSTORM

Work with a partner. Imagine you work for TWC Management Consultancy. What practical ideas can you suggest they implement to ensure all staff are prepared and support the company changes? Think of at least four ideas.

PLAN

Plan the main body and conclusion of TWC Management Consultancy's report to Buckson's. The main body will include your recommendations. Decide what headings to use for each section of your report.

WRITE

Write the report using an appropriate layout. Include participle clauses and a variety of punctuation. Make sure your report is clear and concise. Write around 300 words.

SHARE

Exchange your report with a partner. Read the checklist below and give feedback to your partner.
- Has your partner used an appropriate report layout?
- Has your partner explained his/her suggestions clearly and concisely?
- Has your partner used any participle clauses appropriately?
- Has your partner used a variety of punctuation?

REWRITE AND EDIT

Consider your partner's comments and rewrite your report.

STUDY SKILLS Editing your work

Getting started

Discuss these questions with a partner.

1 Why is it important to revise and edit your work after you've written it?
2 How much time do you spend editing your work?
3 What approach do you take when you edit your work?

Scenario

Read the scenario and think about what Faisal did right and what he should have done differently.

Consider it

Read the tips about editing and revising your written work. Which strategies do you already use? Which strategies do you think would be useful for you to try? Why?

1 **Fresh eyes.** Leave time between writing and editing your work so that you see things with fresh eyes. It will make it easier to see things that need changing.

2 **First reading.** Think about what you want your piece of writing to say. Read it through and summarize what you have written. Does it match what you want to say? Highlight any sections that need redrafting and spend time working on those.

3 **Second reading.** Read through the text again. This time, consider your reader. Have you supported your arguments effectively? Is it easy to follow? Is it structured appropriately? Is it clearly written?

4 **Proofreading.** Read your text through a final time and concentrate on the language that you have used. Check your grammar and spelling. Think about common errors (*it's/its, they're/there*), but also keep a list of errors you regularly make, such as omitting articles or mistaking verb patterns. Use the spell checker on your computer.

5 **Time management.** Make sure you give yourself enough time to edit and revise your work. You may find that you need to make substantial changes which will impact on your grade. If you leave it until the night before, you may hand in a substandard piece of work.

Over to you

Discuss these questions with a partner.

1 What other things do you think you could do to edit your work?
2 What common grammar errors do you make in your writing? Do you keep a list?
3 What common spelling mistakes do you make? Do you keep a list and learn them so you can spell them better?

Faisal's professor asked him to write a business report on how to motivate staff within an organization. He wrote the report a week before the deadline and then did not look at it again until the night before it had to be handed in.

He read it through once to make sure that all the sections of the report included information that led to the conclusions he had written. He realized that there was a problem with his introduction and it did not quite say what he wanted it to say, so he spent some time working on it. By this time he was feeling tired and so decided that he had worked on the report for long enough. He printed it out and handed it in.

When it was returned, his professor praised the introduction of his report, but pointed out that the report was not structured effectively and it was difficult to understand in places. There were also typos and errors littered throughout it. As a result, his grade was lower than he could have achieved.

Flow

Discussion point

Discuss these questions with a partner.

1 What are some of the world's longest rivers? Where are they?
2 What are some common activities people use rivers for?
3 How do people benefit from rivers? How can rivers threaten or harm people?
Think about:

| energy | floods | the economy | tourism | transportation |

Vocabulary preview

1 **Complete the text with the words in the box.**

> civilisations   commodities   crops   domesticate
> flourish   irrigation   soil   trade

2 **Compare answers with a partner. How would you define each word?**

READING How rivers made civilisation 🇬🇧

Before you read

Do these statements describe ancient Egypt or Mesopotamia? Circle the correct answer with a partner. Then check your answers.

1 The Great Pyramid of Giza was built in **Egypt / Mesopotamia**.
2 Writing was first invented in **Egypt / Mesopotamia**.
3 **Egypt / Mesopotamia** had a strong central government.
4 The culture of **Egypt / Mesopotamia** was generally optimistic.
5 The word **Egypt / Mesopotamia** means 'land between the rivers'.

Answers: Egypt: 1, 3, 4;
Mesopotamia: 2, 5

Global reading

IDENTIFYING LINKS

An important academic skill is the ability to make connections between ideas. This can mean finding links between two ideas in the same text, between the ideas in two different texts, or between an idea in the text and something outside the text in the real world.

Some scholars also attribute the optimistic outlook of the ancient Egyptians to the regularity and stability brought by the Nile …

(Some scholars have linked the idea of the stability of the regular floods of the Nile with the idea that the ancient Egyptians were optimistic.)

Great inventions of ancient (1) _____

The people of ancient Egypt and Mesopotamia were responsible for these and other developments upon which societies today are based.

▲ **Agriculture:** Early people discovered that when rivers flood, they leave behind fertile
   (2) _____ that is excellent for growing
   (3) _____ such as wheat and barley.
▲ (4) _____: Ancient people built networks of canals that brought water to places far from the river. This greatly increased the amount of farmland for agriculture and let them grow materials that could be made into valuable (5) _____ such as rope, boats, and paper.
▲ **Livestock:** Ancient people were the first to
   (6) _____ cows, chickens, goats, and other animals that we still depend on for food today.
▲ (7) _____: The idea that products from one place could be exchanged for those of another land was an ancient invention. This grew the economy, which allowed ancient art and architecture to
   (8) _____.

Read the essay on Egypt and Mesopotamia on pages 90–91 entitled *How rivers made civilisation*, written by a geography student. In what ways are these things linked?

1   The ancient cultures of Egypt, Mesopotamia, China, and Pakistan
2   Rivers and agriculture in ancient Egypt and Mesopotamia
3   Irrigation and the development of writing in Mesopotamia
4   Ancient Mesopotamian culture and modern Iraqi culture
5   The Nile and trade in ancient Egypt
6   The Sahara desert and the political state of Egypt

Critical thinking skill

■ IDENTIFYING LOGICAL FALLACIES

A logical fallacy is an error in reasoning. If an argument contains a fallacy, it is not valid, although the conclusion it supports may still be accurate or true. In your university courses, you will sometimes be assigned texts to read whose arguments have weaknesses similar to the ones below, and professors will expect you to notice and discuss them.

- **Argument from ignorance:** Saying that something must be true only because it has not been proven false.

  No one saw him leave his house, so he must have been home all night.

- **Confusing correlation and causation:** Saying that because two things often happen together or at the same time (correlation), one must cause the other (causation).

  Most drivers involved in car accidents are right-handed; therefore, being right-handed causes car accidents.

- **After, therefore, because:** Saying that because X happened before Y, X caused Y.

  Test scores increased after the school repainted the hallways, suggesting that changes in color have a direct effect on student performance.

1   Look at the examples of logical fallacies in italics in the box above. With a partner, explain in your own words why each argument is not valid.

2   Each of these lines from *How rivers made civilisation* is making an argument with a logical fallacy. Read the paragraphs these lines come from, then match them with the correct summary of the argument below.

___ 1   "The only thing that made all of this possible was water." (para. 1)
___ 2   "It is probably not a coincidence that after these conflicts arose, Mesopotamians developed the world's first systems of writing and laws." (para. 4)
___ 3   "Since no evidence has yet emerged to disprove this connection, it remains a reasonable and likely explanation." (para. 10)

a   Because writing and laws first appeared after the development of irrigation, irrigation must be the reason why they were invented.
b   We can assume that the Nile deeply influenced Egyptian culture since nothing to disprove this has been found.
c   Rivers are the main cause of civilization because so many civilizations began near major rivers.

3   What kind of logical fallacy can you find in each argument in exercise 2?

Developing critical thinking

Discuss these questions in a group.

Make a list of developments or inventions that are vital parts of any civilization. Why is each one important? Which one is most important?

How rivers made civilisation 🇬🇧

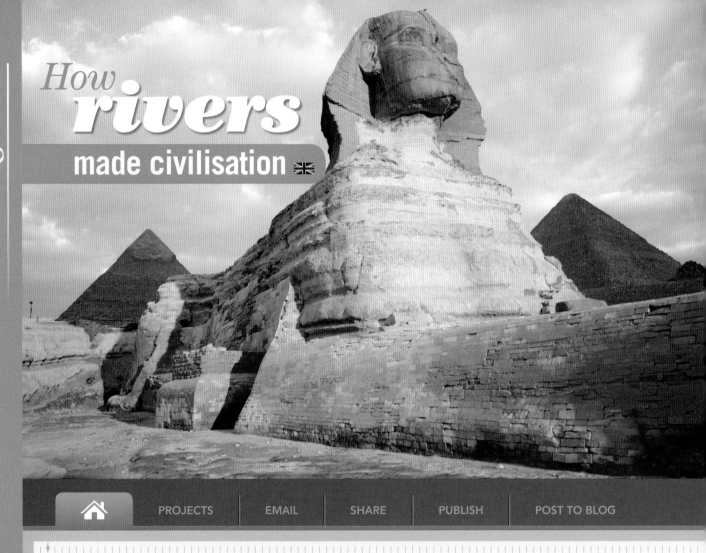

PROJECTS | EMAIL | SHARE | PUBLISH | POST TO BLOG

¹ Around 8,000 years ago, new civilisations began to flourish all over the world. In present-day Egypt, China, Iraq, and Pakistan, these groups developed innovations that are the building blocks of human societies today: writing, the wheel, irrigation, trade, laws, and more. The only thing that made all of this possible was water. More specifically, these civilisations arose from rivers: the Nile in Egypt, the Yellow River in China, the Tigris and Euphrates in Mesopotamia, and the Indus in Pakistan. The rivers and their surrounding geography provided people with fertile soil for agriculture, valuable trade routes, and a base for the first real cities. The rivers may even have had an effect on these early peoples' beliefs and worldviews. This essay will examine two significant river valley civilisations—Egypt and Mesopotamia—and the impact of rivers and other aspects of geography on their rise.

Mesopotamia and the Fertile Crescent

² Mesopotamia was never a single, unified country; the name comes from a Greek word that means 'land between the rivers' (Wood 2010). In reality, the region was a loose collection of cultures that rose and fell over the millennia, starting around 8,000 years ago, and were often at war with each other (Collon 2011, Wood 2010). They included Sumeria, Assyria, Akkadia, Babylon, and many others (Penn Museum 2012). Despite this disunity, the cultures of Mesopotamia were the first to develop agriculture, domesticate livestock, invent the wheel, build cities, and write literature (Collon 2011).

³ The rivers of Mesopotamia were the Tigris and the Euphrates, flowing through present-day Iraq and emptying in the Persian Gulf. (They also flowed through parts of Turkey, Syria, and Iran.) In this area, which today we know as the 'fertile crescent', the rivers flooded violently and unpredictably, but the soil left behind by the floods made for excellent farmland for wheat, barley, and dates (Metz 1988). The marshes around the rivers were a source of fish and birds to eat, and reeds growing in the marshes could be used to weave mats and roofs (Penn Museum 2012). These commodities had great value to people around the region. As a result, within a few thousand years, the Mesopotamians had also established trade routes with Iran, India, and the regions to the north. These routes partly made use of the Tigris and Euphrates, but were mostly overland (Penn Museum 2012).

⁴ Since the Mesopotamians were organised in large cities, some as large as 100,000 people, there was a labour force large enough to build large-scale irrigation projects. This resulted in more farmland and more food, but also in disputes over land and water (Wood 2010). It is probably not a coincidence that after these conflicts arose, Mesopotamians developed the world's first systems of writing and laws. Without irrigation, they might never have been invented.

5 Although these cultures flourished, the geography of Mesopotamia left them vulnerable. The floods that made their civilisation possible also brought much suffering. The rivers did not flood on a predictable schedule and could cause serious harm. Despite the floods, the climate was not rainy and water was scarce, leading to constant conflicts. There were no mountains, deserts, or other natural barriers to keep outside groups away, or to prevent one city within Mesopotamia from attacking another (Wood 2010). Not surprisingly, the outlook on life that resulted from these circumstances was deeply pessimistic. Ancient Babylonian literature contains a great deal of sorrow and mourning—a trait that some Arab observers say is still present in the culture of modern-day Iraq.

Egypt and the Nile River

6 Around 9,000 years ago, the region that is now the Sahara desert was actually relatively rainy and green. This rainy period ended about 6,000 years ago, however, giving rise to massive desertification in northern Africa (Carey 2006). As the Sahara desert expanded, the people of northern Africa migrated to the Nile River valley. Believed to be the world's longest river, the Nile flows over 6,600 kilometres through ten nations. One of its main branches, the Blue Nile, begins in the highlands of Ethiopia; summer thunderstorms here cause yearly floods thousands of kilometres downstream in Egypt. These floods deposit rich soil on the land near the river, resulting in fertile farmland (Hays 2008).

7 The ancient Egyptians took advantage of this new farmland in a number of ways. They grew enough wheat and barley to meet their own needs, with a significant surplus to keep on hand for lean years, or to trade. The Nile also provided fish to eat and a marshy hunting ground for birds (Baines 2011). Over several centuries, the ancient Egyptians created irrigation systems and used the resulting increase in the amount of farmland to cultivate crops that were valuable for trade, such as flax, which could be made into rope or linen cloth, or papyrus, which was used to make boats, mats, and even paper (Baines 2011).

8 The Nile not only gave ancient Egyptians valuable commodities for trade but also served as the trading route itself. The Nile linked Egypt to the peoples of both sub-Saharan Africa and the Mediterranean. Being better situated and more advanced, the ancient Egyptians dominated trade in both regions (Baines 2011). The river and the surrounding landscape also protected the ancient Egyptians. The Nile Delta, where the river meets the Mediterranean, was very difficult for an invading army to march through, while crossing the Sahara itself was simply unthinkable (Baines 2011). As a result of this prosperity and stability, ancient Egypt grew into a large, politically unified state, perhaps the first of its kind in history, ruled by pharaohs whose iconic pyramids we marvel at to this day. Another factor in this stability was the predictable regularity of the floods and their relatively gentle nature (Baines 2011). This allowed the Egyptians to plan for the future without the fear of disruptions or natural disasters that could upset the political order.

9 Any civilisation which owed so much to a body of water would undoubtedly have a deep cultural connection with it, and many believe the same was true of the ancient Egyptians. In fact, because the Nile had such a profound influence on almost every aspect of their culture, the Egyptians often seemed barely to take notice of the river, just as fish in the sea seem unaware of the water all around them. For example, the Egyptians had no name for the Nile in their language, simply referring to it as 'the river', and the Nile is not directly represented in their mythology (Baines 2011).

10 However, in other respects, the Nile played a significant part in Egyptian culture. Their calendar was based on the annual floods (Baines 2011). The pyramids of Egypt were all built on the same side of the Nile. Some scholars attribute the optimistic outlook of the ancient Egyptians to the regularity and stability brought by the Nile and the landscape around it (Wood 2010). At any rate, since no evidence has yet emerged to disprove this connection, it remains a reasonable and likely explanation.

11 All living things depend on water for survival, but what history reveals is that civilisation as we know it also owes its existence to water, and particularly to the ancient river valley civilisations of Mesopotamia and Egypt. By taking advantage of the ideal conditions these rivers created for agriculture, trade, and—in the case of Egypt—unity and stability, these ancient peoples laid the foundations of our societies today: writing, laws, agriculture, calendars, trade, and much more.

Sources

Baines, John. 'The Story of the Nile', bbc.co.uk/history/ancient/egyptians/nile_01.shtml. 17 February 2011

Carey, Bjorn. 'Sahara Desert Was Once Lush and Populated', livescience.com/4180-sahara-desert-lush-populated.html. 20 July 2006

Collon, Dominique. 'Mesopotamia', bbc.co.uk/ancient/cultures/mesopotamia. 1 July 2011

Gearon, Eamonn. *The Sahara: A Cultural History*. Oxford University Press, 2011

Hays, Jeffrey. 'Geography, land, nature and weather in Egypt', Factsanddetails.com/world.php?itemid=1924&catid=56&subcatid=364. 2008–8012

Metz, Helen Chapin ed. *Iraq: A Country Study*, Washington, DC: Federal Research Division of the Library of Congress, 1988

University of Pennsylvania Museum of Archaeology and Anthropology, 'Iraq's Ancient Past', www.penn.museum/sites/iraq. Accessed July 2012

Wood, Michael. 'Mesopotamia: Birthplace of civilisation', *Guardian*, 10 November 2010

ACADEMIC KEYWORDS

arise	(v)	/əˈraɪz/
existence	(n)	/ɪgˈzɪstəns/
society	(n)	/səˈsaɪəti/

Language development

VERBS AND EXPRESSIONS WITH PREPOSITIONS

There are a large number of verbs and expressions that are followed by a specific preposition. As you read, it is helpful to note down these verbs and expressions and learn them.

In many cases, a verb can go with different prepositions, but the meaning often changes.

Large-scale irrigation **resulted in** *more farmland.* (*result in* = cause)

A pessimistic outlook **resulted from** *these circumstances.* (*result from* = be caused by)

1 **Circle the correct preposition to complete the sentences. The verbs and expressions are all found in *How rivers made civilisation*.**

  1 The invention of writing **had an effect** *at* / *on* people's powers of memory.
  2 Advanced societies **arose** *to* / *from* several different river valleys in history.
  3 Mesopotamia was located mostly in what is now **known** *as* / *for* Iraq.
  4 The stone found in Egypt **made** *of* / *for* excellent building materials.
  5 The Egyptians **made use** *of* / *for* the Nile as a trade route and a food source.
  6 The growth of the Sahara **resulted** *in* / *from* a large migration to the Nile.
  7 Population growth can **lead** *in* / *to* conflicts over land and resources.
  8 Egypt's political stability **resulted** *in* / *from* its secure location.
  9 Increased trade in the ancient world **gave rise** *to* / *from* greater power and prestige for ancient Egypt.

2 **Complete these lines with a preposition. Then find the lines in *How rivers made civilisation* and check your answers.**

  1 … the rivers and their surrounding geography provided people _____ fertile soil … (para. 1)
  2 … the ancient Egyptians took advantage _____ this new farmland … (para. 7)
  3 … whose iconic pyramids we marvel _____ to this day. (para. 8)
  4 … seemed barely to take notice _____ the river … (para. 9)
  5 Some scholars also attribute the optimistic outlook of the ancient Egyptians _____ the regularity and stability … (para. 10)
  6 … civilisation as we know it also owes its existence _____ water … (para. 11)

EXPRESSING CAUSALITY

There are many ways to show a cause and effect relationship between two people, things, or ideas.

- Use *because*, *so*, *as*, or *since* before a clause.
  Since the Mesopotamians were in cities, there was a large labour force.
  Ancient Egypt flourished **because** the Nile provided food, wealth, and security.
- Use *as a result* or *consequently* at the beginning of a sentence or after a semicolon.
  As a result, the Mesopotamians established trade routes with Iran and India.
  Mesopotamia was vulnerable to invasion; **consequently**, warfare was common.
- Use expressions with prepositions such as *result from*, *lead to*, and *have an effect on*.
  The outlook on life that **resulted from** these circumstances was deeply pessimistic.
- Use adjectives that show causality, such as *resulting*, *resultant*, *consequent*, and *ensuing*.
  They created irrigation systems and used the **resulting** increase in farmland to grow flax.
- Use noun phrases such as *a factor in*, *a cause of*, *impact of A on B*, *a consequence of*, or *role in*.
  This essay will examine **the impact of** rivers **on** the rise of Egypt and Mesopotamia.

1 **Use the expressions in parentheses to write sentences that show cause and effect relationships. Put the cause and effect in the correct order.**

1 excellent farmland / the Nile's yearly floods (give rise to)
   The Nile's yearly floods gave rise to excellent farmland.

2 the development of money / more efficient trade (result in)

3 Egypt was the strongest culture in the region / it dominated trade (as)

4 the ancient Egyptians' outlook on life / the gentle nature of the Nile's floods (have an effect on)

5 conflict was common in Mesopotamia / water was scarce (consequently)

6 a lack of natural barriers to invasion / political instability in Mesopotamia (result from)

7 disputes over land / the development of writing and laws (a factor in)

8 rivers / rise of civilization / is hard to overstate (the impact of … on …)

2 **Write one or two sentences to answer each question. Use the expressions in the skills box to show cause and effect relationships.**

1 What had a greater **impact on** society, writing or the wheel?

2 What are some positive and negative things that have **resulted from** trade?

3 What good and bad things have **arisen from** the growth of cities?

4 Can conflict between people or groups ever **lead to** anything good?

5 How can geography be **a factor in** the development of a culture?

3 **Compare your answers to exercise 2 with a partner.**

WRITING A cause and effect essay

You are going to learn about writing effective concluding paragraphs that will help readers better appreciate your ideas. You are then going to use this skill to write about the connection between the geography of a place and its history and culture.

Writing skill

WRITING EFFECTIVE CONCLUSIONS

In academic writing, an effective concluding paragraph always restates the main idea and the key arguments that support it. In addition, you can use some of the following techniques to help your ideas leave a stronger impression in the minds of your readers.

- Restate your main idea and supporting points in a new way. Don't repeat them word for word from earlier in the essay.

- Show how your topic or main idea is relevant to the concerns of readers today.

  Almost every part of our daily lives—from traffic laws to text messages to imported fruits and vegetables—has its roots in the early river valley civilizations.

- Extend the main idea by discussing its implications. For example, think of things that people should or should not do in light of this idea.

  The history of these civilizations highlights the importance of the environment to human societies; we still depend on rivers today, and ought to treat them with greater care.

1 The paragraph below is the conclusion to *How rivers made civilisation*. Which of the tips in the box did the writer follow?

All living things depend on water for survival, but what history reveals is that civilisation as we know it also owes its existence to water, and particularly to the ancient river valley civilisations of Mesopotamia and Egypt. By taking advantage of the ideal conditions these rivers created for agriculture, trade, and—in the case of Egypt—unity and stability, these ancient peoples laid the foundations of our societies today: writing, laws, agriculture, calendars, trade, and much more.

2 Work with a partner. Write a new conclusion to *How rivers made civilisation*. Use as many of the tips in the box as you can.

3 Compare your conclusion with others. Choose the most effective conclusion and read it to the class.

WRITING TASK

You are going to write about how a place's geography influenced its agriculture, economics, history, and culture. Look at the mind map on the Yellow River valley civilization in China, where Chinese civilization started. Choose a piece of information from the mind map and tell a partner how it is linked to the geography of the region.

Audience:	a teacher and students
Context:	a cause and effect essay
Purpose:	use cause and effect language effectively

There wasn't much trade with outside regions because they were surrounded by mountains and desert.

THE YELLOW RIVER VALLEY CIVILIZATION

Geography
- Flows through central China
- 5,464 km long
- Called "yellow" because full of soil
- Violent, unpredictable floods
- Surrounded by mountains and desert

Agriculture
- Floods created excellent farmland
- Developed irrigation to expand farmland
- Main crops = wheat and barley
- Domesticated livestock for food

Economics
- Was most prosperous region of China
- Not much trade with outside regions

Culture
- Advanced technology: pottery, boats, silk, use of bronze
- Also invented fireworks and their own form of paper
- Isolated from world outside China
- Saw themselves as center of world; "China" means "middle kingdom"

History and Politics
- Called "cradle of Chinese civilization"
- Civilization started about 4,000 years ago
- United different ethnic groups along river
- Ruled by king; created first bureaucracy

BEIJING

CHINA

BRAINSTORM

Think of places you know whose history, economics, or culture have been influenced by their geography.

PLAN

In preparation for your essay, choose one place and reflect on it. (If you prefer, you can use the mind map to write about the Yellow River valley civilization.) Think about how its geography influenced its agriculture, economics, history, and culture.

Create a mind map or an outline for your essay.

WRITE

Write your essay in around 300 words. Include verbs and expressions with prepositions and expressions of causality. Use the tips for writing an effective conclusion.

SHARE

Exchange essays with a partner. As you read your partner's essay, think about the following points:
- Does the essay show cause and effect relationships between the geography of a place and its history, economics, or culture?
- Did the writer correctly use expressions of causality and verbs and expressions with prepositions?
- Is the conclusion effective? How could it be improved?

REWRITE AND EDIT

Consider your partner's comments and rewrite your essay.

Assuming a causal link

by Stella Cottrell

It is flawed reasoning to assume that because two things are found together, or occur at the same time, there must be a link between them. One example of this is assuming a link to be one of cause and effect: that one thing must be the 'cause' of another, or, in effect, jumping to a particular kind of conclusion.

Example 1

Wherever dinosaur imprints are found in rocks, there are geologists around. Therefore, geologists must make the imprints.

The assumption here is that as geologists and dinosaur prints occur in the same place, the geologists create the prints. The underlying assumption is that the dinosaur prints must be fake. If this were not the case, the author couldn't draw the conclusion that geologists must make the prints. The more logical assumption is that the prints attract the geologists as they are a natural subject for geologists to research when they are dating rocks. Other evidence is likely to prove they pre-dated the arrival of the geologists by a great many years.

Example 2

The entire family was ill last night. They all ate fish at the restaurant yesterday. Therefore, the fish must have been contaminated.

Here, the cause of the illness is linked to eating fish. The underlying assumption is that nothing else could have made the family ill. Without this assumption, the author couldn't draw the conclusion that the fish was bad. More evidence than this would be needed to prove that bad fish was the cause of the illness, such as:

- whether anybody else who ate fish from the same batch became ill;
- what the nature of the illness is;

- what else might have caused the illness;
- an examination of the fish remains.

Activity

For each passage, identify the assumed causal link or links.

Passage 1

Life expectancy is much higher in Western countries than in the past. Obesity is also much higher. Therefore, obesity must increase our life expectancy.

Passage 2

A prisoner who protested his innocence by sitting on the prison roof has been released. This is the second time that a prisoner who has protested in this way has been released. Roof-top protests must be a good way of securing release from the prison.

Passage 3

The man's body was found in the kitchen. A bloody knife was found nearby. The lock on the door had been broken. Somebody must have broken in and killed the man.

Conflict

READING	Identifying causes
CRITICAL THINKING	Identifying humor
LANGUAGE DEVELOPMENT	Phrasal nouns Verb patterns
WRITING	The writer's voice

Discussion point

Discuss these questions with a partner.

1 What are some topics that people often argue about? Make a list. What sorts of people argue about these things (friends, colleagues, families, husbands and wives, etc.)?

2 Different people have different conflict styles. Think of people you know who do the things below when they argue.

> become loud and emotional   seem to enjoy conflict
> stay calm and quiet   try to avoid conflict

3 If two people have a serious disagreement that they cannot solve on their own, what else can they do?

Vocabulary preview

Read the sentences below. Which of the bold words can be used to talk about:

a   a fight, argument, or conflict?   c   a solution to a conflict?

b   an angry emotion?   d   a positive personality trait?

1   Because our downtown has very few parking spaces, angry **disputes** between drivers are very common.

2   Both sides shook hands and apologized after finding a **resolution** to their conflict.

3   The company was forced to apologize and pay a fine, so **justice** was done.

4   Now that everyone shares the chores equally, there is **harmony** at home.

5   Mark ignored Tim's insult in order to avoid having a **confrontation**.

6   Management's decision to reduce pay led to a **clash** with angry workers.

7   Julia was **seething** when she learned she hadn't been invited to the party.

8   **Sincerity** is an important quality in a leader; you must mean what you say.

READING   Culture and conflict

Before you read

Discuss with a partner. Who does most of the chores in your home? Do you and your family ever argue about this?

Global reading

1   **Read the humorous business magazine article entitled *Culture and conflict*, on pages 100–101. Complete the summary of some of the main concepts in the essay with the words in the box.**

diffuseness	high-context	low-context	monochronic	polychronic	specificity

In *Culture and conflict*, Paul Wright describes how (1) _____ speakers rely on words to deliver their message, whereas (2) _____ speakers also rely on gestures, the situation, and shared understandings. He explains how, in (3) _____ cultures, people value relationships over schedules, but in (4) _____ cultures, schedules and punctuality are very important. He also describes how people who value (5) _____ solve conflicts in ways that save face for others and repair relationships. On the other hand, those who value (6) _____ tend to focus on a single, central aspect of a conflict.

Business Monthly   *June*

IDENTIFYING CAUSES

When reading texts discussing problems and issues, it is important to identify possible causes of these issues.

In many cases, the writer will use cause and effect language to show this. In other cases, you may need to read more carefully or infer meaning that is not overtly stated in order to identify the cause of a problem. These inferred meanings are often about the deeper causes of an issue and are different from the causes that may be apparent on the surface. Examples of deeper causes include differences in values, cultural differences, historical events, and more.

2 **Read the scenarios below. Then read *Culture and conflict* again and identify the main cause of conflict in each one.**

1 The writer is angry that his wife has not washed the dishes.

The writer is a high-context communicator, but his wife has a low-context style. Because of this, he couldn't clearly communicate his concerns about the dishes to his wife.

2 An Asian businessman feels that an American has been rude to him.

3 A British woman is angry that her South American friend is late.

4 A European businessman feels that his counterpart from the Middle East is delaying their meeting for unclear reasons.

3 **Compare your answers with a partner. Which parts of *Culture and conflict* helped you find the answers?**

Critical thinking skill

▌ IDENTIFYING HUMOR ▌

Identifying humor in English is difficult because it often sounds very similar to ordinary language. Common types of English-language humor include:

- **Sarcasm:** Saying one thing, but meaning the opposite.
  *I spent a **delightful** evening changing a flat tire in the pouring rain.*
- **Self-deprecation:** Mocking your flaws while pretending to be proud.
  *I'm a **wonderful** chef if you like burned toast and rubbery eggs.*
- **Understatement:** Using "small" words to describe extremes.
  *It's been **a bit damp**—two straight weeks of rain.*

1 **Find these lines in *Culture and conflict* and read the paragraphs where they appear. Which lines are meant to be humorous? What kinds of humor do they use?**

1 I started dropping what I believed to be very forceful hints, such as saying, "We're nearly out of clean spoons," or looking mournfully at the sink and sighing. (para. 2)

2 This is all in stark contrast to my own family, where our idea of a heated confrontation is to keep quiet for a decade or two … (para. 4)

3 I assumed that my wife shared my beliefs about who should do the dishes and when they should be done … (para. 6)

4 It was a brilliant approach. The only drawback was that my wife … had no idea what I was trying to tell her. (para. 6)

5 On the other hand, the Asian businesspeople may confuse the Americans' directness for rudeness. (para. 7)

6 That's because in the second week I went out and purchased a dishwasher. (para. 11)

Developing critical thinking

Discuss these questions in a group.

1 Do you consider yourself a high-context or low-context person? Are you monochronic or polychronic? Do you value specificity or diffuseness?

2 Think about a conflict you have recently heard about. It could be a conflict between people you know, a conflict in your school or job, or one on a TV show. Do you think the ideas in *Culture and conflict* help to explain it? What other factors are important?

CULTURE *and* CONFLICT

Paul Wright

1 **Whenever I read about conflict, from workplace squabbles to international diplomacy, I think back to the early days of my marriage and a sink full of dirty dishes. After our honeymoon, on our first night in our new home, I cooked a dinner of grilled fish and pasta for my new bride, but she did not wash the dishes.**

2 I couldn't believe it. Weren't we both good, typical Americans who believed in cleaning everything within an inch of its life? And isn't it understood the world over that when someone cooks for you, you have to do the dishes? For the next week, I continued to do the cooking, and she continued not to do the dishes. The dishes stacked higher and higher. I started dropping what I believed to be very forceful hints, such as saying, "We're nearly out of clean spoons," or looking mournfully at the sink and sighing. Yet nothing changed.

3 I was seething inside. Finally, after days of emotional buildup, I decided to teach her a lesson: I would wash the dishes myself! While my wife read in the next room, I snapped on the rubber gloves and clattered and scrubbed as loudly as I could. She looked up from her book and said, with complete sincerity, "Oh! Is it time to do the dishes?"

4 Soon after this, we visited her parents' home, and I observed two things. First, the dirty dishes pile up there and no one minds. Second, and more importantly, the people in my wife's family are incredibly direct. If my mother-in-law has a problem with her husband, he'll be informed of it immediately. There might be a brief outburst of yelling, but then it's all forgotten and everyone is smiling again. This is all in stark contrast to my own family, where our idea of a heated confrontation is to keep quiet for a decade or two, then mutter an indirect reference to the issue while the other party is out of the room.

5 After that visit, I realized there was a very simple reason why my wife hadn't done the dishes: I had never actually asked her to do them. Our situation perfectly illustrates the difference between what the American anthropologist Edward T. Hall, in his landmark book *Beyond Culture*, called *low-context* and *high-context* communication styles. In low-context communication, people speak clearly and directly; they say what they mean and don't expect others to read between the lines. In high-context communication, speakers rely on things other than words, such as body language, gestures, the physical setting, and above all shared knowledge of a culture's unwritten rules.

6 It's easy to see how this applied to my situation at home. As a high-context communicator, I assumed that my wife shared my beliefs about who should do the dishes and when they should be done, so all of my attempts at raising the issue with her were nonverbal and indirect. I expected her to read my mind. It was a brilliant approach. The only drawback was that my wife, coming from a low-context family where everyone freely spoke their mind at any time, had no idea what I was trying to tell her. In fact, she wasn't even *aware* that I was trying to tell her something.

7 Examples abound of clashes between high-context and low-context people. For example, when businesspeople from the U.S.—a typical low-context culture—meet with colleagues from Asia, home to many high-context cultures, there are often misunderstandings. The Americans may fail to understand the nonverbal and contextual cues given by their Asian colleagues. The long silences that are characteristic of high-context communication may also cause the Americans to feel uncomfortable, as if the other party isn't interested in talking with them. On the other hand, the Asian businesspeople may confuse the Americans' directness for rudeness.

8 Another important cultural difference from Hall's work is related to people's concept of time. In *monochronic* cultures such as Britain, time is linear, and people believe in making and adhering to schedules. Meetings start and finish on time, and people stay focused on the scheduled task. On the other hand, in *polychronic* cultures such as South America or the Middle East, time is cyclical. Relationships and personal interaction are considered more important than schedules. Lateness is not an issue, and people may flow from one task to another instead of following an agenda. Many polychronic cultures also feel a stronger connection to events from the distant past, or a greater obligation to future generations, than monochronic cultures do.

9 The potential for conflict here is obvious. According to Hall's theory, when people value their relationships more than time, they will very often clash with people who place greater value on schedules. Take, for example, the slight difference of opinion between the typical Brit, for whom punctuality means everything, and people from places such as South America, where arriving even an hour late is not necessarily considered "late." Similarly, a Middle Eastern businessman may delay an important meeting in order to attend to family matters, and his European counterpart may resent the slowdown, or even wonder whether he is getting the runaround.

10 In addition, individuals and cultures have different ideas about what makes a good resolution to a conflict. Some anthropologists refer to this as a difference between *specificity* and *diffuseness*. People who value specificity want to analyze the conflict and reduce it to a specific problem. In this view, a good resolution brings about justice. It identifies a "right" and "wrong" party and determines an appropriate punishment. On the other hand, people who value diffuseness see conflicts in terms of a broader network of relationships. As a result, they tend to value resolutions that bring about harmony. They want not only to end the present standoff but also to heal the relationships between the different parties involved. This is especially important in cultures that place a high value on saving face, or preserving a person's reputation within his or her own group.

11 These three distinctions are well worth remembering in order to prevent conflicts from happening, or to solve them more easily. Remember also that not every individual in a culture will have the same values. My wife and I were both born and raised in the same city in the U.S., yet we have totally different conceptions of time and communication. In order to truly resolve conflicts and avoid future ones, the key is to understand the other person as an individual and to accept or adapt to his or her ways. In my case, after nearly 12 years of marriage, I've learned to communicate with my wife in a low-context style when needed, and I've also learned that not everything in the household has to follow my schedule. I'm also happy to report that we haven't had a single conflict over who washes the dishes since the first week of our marriage. That's because in the second week I went out and bought a dishwasher.

ACADEMIC KEYWORDS		
belief	(n)	/bɪˈlif/
issue	(n)	/ˈɪʃu/
obvious	(adj)	/ˈɑbviəs/

Language development

PHRASAL NOUNS

Phrasal nouns are nouns created from phrasal verbs, for example: *show off* (v. to boast) and *a showoff* (n. a person who boasts). Phrasal nouns are often written as one word with no spaces. In some cases, the verb and the particle are reversed in a phrasal noun, for example: *upkeep* and *downturn*.

In most cases, a phrasal noun and its related phrasal verb have very similar meanings. In some cases, the meanings are very different, for example: *pay back* (v. to repay a loan) and *payback* (n. revenge).

1 Discuss the meaning of the phrasal verbs in the box with a partner. If needed, use a dictionary to help you.

| break up | build up | burst out | draw back | run around | slow down |

2 Complete the sentences with phrasal nouns formed from the phrasal verbs in exercise 1. Use a dictionary to help you.

1 Conflicts among co-workers are more common when there is a
_____ in the economy and people feel stressed.

2 A _____ of tension between people always leads to conflict, so it is best to express your feelings clearly, honestly, and immediately.

3 The best way to win an argument is to avoid having an angry
_____.

4 The _____ of a large company into smaller divisions is better for business.

5 One _____ to a monochronic attitude is that you are always worried about being on time.

6 If someone won't answer a question directly, he or she is probably giving you the _____ and may even be trying to deceive you.

3 Do the phrasal nouns in exercise 2 have similar meanings to the phrasal verbs in exercise 1? Which ones are different? Which one has a different word order?

4 Discuss the sentences in exercise 2 with a partner. Do you agree with them? How would you change the statements you disagree with?

VERB PATTERNS

In English, certain verbs follow specific patterns with gerunds, infinitives, objects, and prepositions.

- verb + preposition + gerund

  In monochronic cultures, people **believe in making** schedules.

  He **apologized for not arriving** on time to the meeting.

  Other verbs that follow this pattern: *admit to, care about, complain about, concentrate on, confess to, object to, put off, refrain from, succeed in, worry about*

- verb + object + *to* + infinitive

  Long silences may **cause Americans to feel** uncomfortable.

  These misunderstandings **remind us not to take** ourselves so seriously.

  Other verbs that follow this pattern: *allow, ask, beg, command, encourage, expect, force, invite, order, warn*

- verb + object + preposition + gerund

  Remember these points in order to **prevent conflicts from happening**.

  The author **blamed his wife for not doing** the dishes.

  Other verbs that follow this pattern: *accuse someone of, forgive someone for, protect someone/something from, stop someone/something from, thank someone for*

1 **Complete the sentences with the given words. Use the correct verb pattern after the bold verbs. Add prepositions if needed. Use the skills box to help you.**

1 If you argue with a friend, do you usually **apologize** _____ their feelings afterward? (hurt)

2 How much do you **worry** _____ on time to appointments? (not be)

3 If you **invite** _____ dinner at your home at 7:00, at what time should he or she actually arrive? (have, someone)

4 Do your professors usually **encourage** _____ with their ideas or your classmates' answers? (disagree, you)

5 Have people ever **accused** _____ to them when you are having a disagreement with them? (not listen, you)

6 If a classmate or colleague makes a mistake, do you **refrain** _____ them in front of others? (criticize)

7 Is it fair to **expect** _____ his or her voice during an argument? (not raise, someone)

8 Do you find it easy to **forgive** _____ hurtful things to you? (say, someone)

9 What are some ways to **stop** a small disagreement _____ into a serious argument? (turn)

2 **Discuss the questions above with a partner.**

WRITING Analyzing a conflict

You are going to learn about developing your voice as a writer, and you are then going to use this skill to write an essay that analyzes a conflict from different points of view.

Writing skill

> ### THE WRITER'S VOICE
>
> A writer's "voice" is the style he or she writes in, and the personality it shows. Writers vary their voice depending on the audience they are writing for.
>
> - *Going forward, if concerns arise regarding company procedures, please speak to your manager.* (a business email)
> - *A flood of tears gushed down her face; she was bright red with rage.* (a short story)
> - *So sorry I upset you, Tom. Don't know what I said but please forgive me!* (a personal email)
>
> An effective writing voice gives readers the feeling that they are reading the words of a real person, rather than simply reading words on a page. Making this connection with your readers will strengthen your ideas.

1 Read the beginnings of two essays and discuss these questions with a partner.

- Which writer's voice would be more appropriate for an academic paper?
- Which would be better for an essay in a magazine? How do you know?

> 1   When it comes to verbal disputes, it seems that many of us have an extensive and impressive vocabulary for debating, refuting, haranguing, and badgering. Yet when the fight is over, too many people seem to forget entirely about two simple words: "I'm sorry."

> 2   Arguments can be seen as an inevitable feature of close relationships among friends or loved ones. In many cases, one or both parties may attempt to prevail in the dispute through tactics which they later come to regret. This essay will examine various attitudes which speakers may hold toward apologizing and making amends after a dispute has ended.

2 Choose one of the paragraphs in exercise 1 and rewrite it in a new voice to suit one of the following contexts:

- A university student's personal blog
- A corporate training manual
- An email giving advice to a friend
- A newspaper article about a scientific study
- A book giving marriage advice from a psychologist.

3 Compare paragraphs with a partner. Try to guess the situation your partner chose.

WRITING TASK

Write a short essay, using Edward T. Hall's concepts of high-context versus low-context communication and monochronic versus polychronic time to explain the main causes of a conflict. Use an appropriate voice for an academic essay.

Read the model text. Underline the verb patterns with gerunds and infinitives. What adjectives would you use to describe the writer's voice?

Audience:	a university professor
Context:	formative assessment in the form of an essay
Purpose:	use an appropriate voice for an academic essay

The American anthropologist Edward T. Hall's concept of monochronic and polychronic time is a valuable tool for understanding the deeper roots of intercultural conflict. A prime example of this can be found in the difficulties that a U.S. clothing company recently experienced while doing business in South America.

The company initially came to the region with a very monochronic view of time, in which staying on schedule was more important than building relationships. In his first visit, the sales rep spent only a few days in the area. As a result, the trip caused him to feel anxious, as the people he met spent more time socializing than apparently doing business. In actuality, the South American partners saw socializing as part of business.

BRAINSTORM

Make a list of conflicts in the news, in a film or novel, in your personal life, or in the business world. What are some of the causes of each conflict?

PLAN

Choose one of the conflicts and reflect on it. Think about the following, then create an outline for your essay.

- Who is involved in the conflict?
- In what way are each side's values and ideas similar or different?
- How do these differences relate to Hall's ideas about communication and time?
- Was the conflict resolved? How? Was it a good resolution? Why or why not?
- What would be the best way to resolve the conflict? Why?

WRITE

Write your essay in around 300 words. Use verb patterns with gerunds and infinitives. As you write, make sure your voice is appropriate for an academic essay.

SHARE

Exchange essays with a partner. As you read your partner's essay, consider the following points:

- Does the essay describe the conflict and analyze its causes?
- Does the essay describe the best way to resolve the conflict?
- Is the writer's voice appropriate for an academic essay?

REWRITE AND EDIT

Consider your partner's comments and rewrite your essay.

Relevant and irrelevant evidence

by Stella Cottrell

Relevance and irrelevance

Relevant evidence is that which is necessary to give a good understanding of the issues. An author can provide evidence that:

(1) supports the conclusion;

(2) is relevant to the subject, but which may not be relevant to the conclusion: in this case, the evidence might even contradict the conclusion;

(3) is relevant neither to the conclusion nor to the subject.

Example 1

People need to improve their understanding of how language works so that they can use it more effectively. Research studies (Bloggs, 2003; Bloggs, 2006) show that the study of a foreign language improves our understanding of the structure of language, providing a way of comparing different language structures. Therefore, people who only speak one language should be encouraged to study a second language.

Here, the research evidence about the benefits of studying a foreign language is relevant to the conclusion that people who speak only one language should be encouraged to study a second language.

Example 2

People need to improve their understanding of how language works so that they can use it more effectively. Research studies (Bloggs, 2003; Bloggs, 2006) show that many people cannot describe the different components of their own language. A surprising number of people have difficulties remembering the rules even of their mother tongue. Therefore, people who only speak one language should be encouraged to study a second language.

Here the evidence that people have difficulties in their own language could be interpreted to suggest that people who have difficulties with one language should not be encouraged to learn a second. The evidence is relevant to the debate, but does not support the argument. Further information would be needed to support the conclusion.

Example 3

People need to improve their understanding of how language works so that they can use it more effectively. Research studies (Bloggs, 2003; Bloggs, 2006) show people can recognise concepts in a foreign language even when there is no word for that concept in their mother tongue. Therefore, people who only speak one language should be encouraged to study a second language.

Here, the evidence about recognising concepts in a foreign language is loosely related to the topic about languages. However, it has a completely different focus. It has no apparent relevance to the debate about using language effectively or the conclusion that people should learn a second language in order to use language more effectively.

Relevance to the conclusion

In considering whether evidence is relevant, your main focus should be on whether the conclusion would be different if that evidence (or reason) was different or not available.

Check

When evaluating an argument, check:

- Is the evidence relevant to the topic?
- Is it needed to substantiate the reasoning?
- Does it make a difference to the conclusion?
- If so, does it support it or contradict it?
- Is the evidence needed to substantiate interim conclusions?

The phrases below give common ways of expressing useful functions.
Use them to help you as you're completing the *Discussion points* and
Developing critical thinking activities.

Asking for clarification

Sorry, can you explain that some more?
Could you say that another way?
When you say ..., do you mean ...?
Sorry, I don't follow that.
What do you mean?

Asking for repetition

Could you repeat that, please?
I'm sorry, I didn't catch that.
Could you say that again?

When you don't know the meaning of a word

What does ... mean?
Sorry, I'm not sure what ... means.

Working with a partner

Would you like to start?
Shall I go first?
Shall we do this one first?
Where do you want to begin?

Giving opinions

I think that ...
It seems to me that ...
In my opinion ...
As I see it ...

Agreeing and disagreeing

I know what you mean.
That's true.
You have a point there.
Yes. I see what you're saying, but ...
I understand your point, but ...
I don't think that's true.

Asking for opinions

Do you think ...?
Do you feel ...?
What do you think about ...?
How about you, Jennifer? What do you think?
What about you?
Does anyone have any other ideas?
Do you have any thoughts on this?

Asking for more information

In what way?
Why do you think that?
Can you give an example?

Not giving a strong preference

It doesn't matter to me.
I don't really have a strong preference.
I've never really thought about that.
Either is fine.

Expressing interest

I'd like to hear more about that.
That sounds interesting.
How interesting!
Tell me more about that.

Giving reasons

This is ... because ...
This has to be ... because ...
I think ... because ...

Checking understanding

Do you know what I mean?
Do you see what I'm saying?
Are you following me?

Putting things in order

This needs to come first because ...
I think this is the most/least important because ...
For me, this is the most/least relevant because ...

Preventing interruptions

Excuse me, I wasn't finished.
If I could just finish what I was saying ...
Let me just finish this, please.
I haven't finished my thought/sentence.

Buying time

Let me think about that for a moment.
Let me gather my thoughts.
Just a minute. I need to think about that.

Clarifying

That's not exactly what I meant.
Sorry, I wasn't clear. Let me put it another way.
That isn't what I was trying to say.

Writing task peer review checklist

Use the checklist below as you read over your partner's work.

PROCESS WRITING CHECKLIST

1 Does the composition have these things:
- [ ] a title
- [ ] an introduction, a body, and a conclusion
- [ ] appropriate punctuation

2 Write the thesis statement here:

_____

_____

3 Underline the topic sentence in each paragraph. (If you can't find the topic sentence in any paragraphs, write the numbers of those paragraphs here: _____)

4 Is the author's position on the issue/topic clear?

5 Write any target vocabulary from the unit here:

_____

6 Draw a star by one or two sentences that you especially liked. What did you especially like about these sentences?

7 Are sources provided for factual statements?

8 Write one question about the content/ideas of the composition for the author:

_____

The publishers would like to thank the following for their thoughtful insights and perceptive comments during the development of the material:

Reviewers

Belgium

Sylviane Granger, at CECL, University of Louvain
Magali Paquot

Egypt

Dr Gaber Khalil, AUC, Cairo
Heidi Omara

Germany

John Nixon at Universität Stuttgart

Ireland

Fiodhna Gardiner-Hyland at University of Limerick

Japan

Robert Morton at Chuo University
Lesley Burda Ito

Oman

Mutaz Abumuaath at Nizwa College of Technology, Nizwa

Qatar

Jane Hoelker at Qatar University, Foundation English

Russia

Tatyana Gromoglasova at the Siberian Institute of Management, Novosibirsk

Saudi Arabia

Dr Mohammed Al-Ahaydib and Dr Mohammed Hamdan at Imam Muhammad Ibn Saud University
Dr William Frawley, Education Experts

South Korea

Yoonji Kim, and Da Young Song at the Konkuk University Language Institute
Jina Kwon at Seoul National University

Taiwan

Laura Wang at Chung Yuan Christian University
Regina Jan at Lunghwa University of Science and Technology
Kitty Chu, Jessie Huang, Jenny Jen, and Wenyau Keng at the National Central University, Language Center

Sandrine Ting at the Department of Applied Foreign Language, St. John's University

Thailand

Wanpen Chaikitmongkol, Jindarat De Vleeschauwer, and Sonhsi Wichaidit at the English Division, Department of Western Languages and Humanities, Chiang Mai University

Turkey

Merve Oflaz at Bahçeşehir University
Şahika Özkan-Tuğba Kın-Yadigar Aslan, Didem Gümüşlüoğlu, Meltem Sarandal, and Sibel Weeks at Doğuş University, İstanbul
Sevil Altikulaçoğlu, Sühendan Semine Er, Şerife Ersöz, and Fatma Ünveren Gürocak at Gazi University
Deniz Ateşok at Istanbul Bilgi University
Ebru Yamaç at Maltepe University
Aybike Oğuz at Özyeğin University

United Arab Emirates

Paul Barney, Doug Henderson, and Danielle Norris at Higher Colleges of Technology, Al Ain

United Kingdom

Nick Hillman at Anglia Ruskin University
Heather Abel and Richard Hillman at Bell London
Edward Bressan, Sara Hannam, and Stacey Hughes at Oxford Brookes University
Sally Morris, Ian Pople, and Simon Raw at University of Manchester
Averil Bolster and Peter Levrai at University of Nottingham, Ningbo
Jonathan Hadley
Jane Neill at University of Gloucester

United States

Gail Schafers at Fontbonne University
Carole Mawson at Stanford University
Denise Mussman at University of Missouri
Abby Brown

Macmillan Education
4 Crinan Street, London N1 9XW
A division of Macmillan Publishers Limited

Companies and representatives throughout the world

ISBN 978-0-230-43008-2

Text, design and illustration © Macmillan Publishers Limited 2014
Written by Mike Boyle and Lindsay Warwick
Series Consultant Dorothy E. Zemach

The authors have asserted their rights to be identified as the authors
of this work in accordance with the Copyright, Designs and Patents
Act 1988.

First published 2014

Designed by emc design ltd
Illustrated by emc design ltd
Cover design by emc design ltd
Cover illustration/photograph by Thinkstock/iStockphoto
Picture research by Emily Taylor

The Academic Keyword List (AKL) was designed by Magali Paquot at
the Centre for English Corpus Linguistics, Université catholique de
Louvain (Belgium) within the framework of a research project led by
Professor Sylviane Granger.

http://www.uclouvain.be/en-372126.html

Authors' acknowledgements

Mike Boyle
I am very grateful to Dorothy Zemach and the entire Macmillan
Education team for their guidance and insightful comments, and for
the many ways in which they have improved my work. I would also
like to thank my wife for all of her support and encouragement.

Lindsay Warwick
I would like to give huge thanks to Dorothy Zemach and the
Macmillan Education editorial team for their incredibly helpful
suggestions; my colleagues at Bell for continued inspiration; my family
and Alex for their support and patience.

The authors and publishers would like to thank the following for
permission to reproduce their material:

Alamy/Blend Images p15, Alamy/Joe Fox p34, Alamy/Alan
Gignouxp74, Alamy/Geraint Lewis p73, Alamy/Keith Morris p11,
Alamy/Motoring Picture Library p77, Alamy/Paul Springett B p54;

Axiom Photographic/Peter McBride p98;

Corbis/Andrew Aitchison/In Pictures p50, Corbis/ArabianEye
p26, Corbis/Richard Ashworth/Robert Harding World Imagery
p89, Corbis/Eric Audras/PhotoAlto p12, Corbis/DPA p19, Corbis/
Jose Fuste Raga p88, Corbis/Christopher Morris p17, Corbis/Steve
Raymer/National Geographic Society pp70–71, Corbis/Bertrand
Rieger/Hemis p94, Corbis/STR/epa p51, Corbis/Tetra Images p104,
Corbis/Dana Tynan p30, Corbis/Ken Welsh/Design Pics p69;

FotoLibra/Walter Rawlings p95, FotoLibra /Rodger Shagam p48,
FotoLibra/Sue Walker p20;

Getty Images/AFP p21, Getty Images/ArabianEye pp5(br), 86, Getty
Images/Cultura RF p31, Getty Images/DeAgostini p92, Getty Images/
Dem10 p67, Getty Images/Flickr RF pp62–63, Getty Images/Jan
Galbraith p27, Getty Images/Glow Images p105, Getty Images/Image
Source p33, Getty Images/Jupiterimages p79, Getty Images/Clarissa
Leahy p100, Getty Images/Lonely Planet Images pp23, 58, Getty
Images/Debra McClinton p28(br), Getty Images/Roy Mehta p9, Getty
Images/PeskyMonkey p60, Getty Images/Nullplus p64, Getty Images/
OrangeDukeProductions p102, Getty Images/Harry Sieplinga/HMS
Images p28(tr), Getty Images/Vetta p87, Getty Images/Mehmed
Zelkovic p57;

National Geographic/Dmitry Dolzhanskiy p47, National
Geographic/Frans Lanting p97;

PhotoDisc p90;

Plain Picture p66, Plain Picture/Amana Images p52, Plain Picture/
Cultura pp16, 46, 82, 85, 101, Plain Picture/Christian Diehl p7, Plain
Picture/Maskot p45, Plain Picture/Naturbild p42, Plain Picture/
Tranquillium p35, Plain Picture/Westend61 pp5(cl), 40-41, Plain
Picture/Allard de Witte pp5(tr), 37;

Press Association Images/AP pp25, 65

The authors and publishers are grateful for permission to reprint the
following copyright material:

Material from *Critical Thinking Skills 2ⁿᵈ edn 2011* by author Stella
Cottrell, copyright © Stella Cottrell 2011, first published by Palgrave
Macmillan 2005, reproduced with permission of the publisher;

Direct quotation by Professor Elizabeth Loftus, reprinted with
approval;

Direct quotation by Professor K. David Harrison, reprinted with
approval;

Material from website www.ling.hawaii.edu, reprinted with approval.

Printed and bound in Thailand

2018 2017 2016 2015 2014
10 9 8 7 6 5 4 3 2 1

Recommended system requirements for the *Skillful* Digibook

Windows	XP SP3 / Vista / Windows 7 / Windows 8
CPU Speed	Core 2 Duo, 2.33 GHz
Browser	Explorer 8 / Explorer 9 / Firefox / Chrome

Macintosh	OS 10.6 / 10.7 / 10.8
CPU Speed	Core 2 Duo, 1.83 GHz
Browser	Firefox

Additional recommended system requirements

ONLINE VERSION

Free RAM: 500 MB
Display: 1024 x 768 pixels, 32-bit colour
Add-ins: Adobe Acrobat Reader, Flash Player 10.1
Broadband connection: For Authentication / Registration / Updates

INSTALLABLE VERSION

Hard Disk: Min. 2 GB (install drive) and 2 GB (system drive)
Free RAM: 2 GB
Display: 1024 × 768 pixels, 32-bit colour
Add-ins: Adobe Acrobat Reader, Flash Player 11.5, Java 1.6 JRE
Administration rights: One-time, to install the software
Broadband connection: For Authentication / Registration / Updates / Download

Note: Network administrators should visit www.skillfuldigibooks.com/help.html for detailed information regarding Proxy/Firewall/Antivirus settings before they install any digibooks

This software is licensed for use by one user and can be installed on a maximum of one machine.

Product Activation

1   Type www.skillfuldigibooks.com into your Internet browser.

2   Click "Enter your token details."

3   You need your access token code, printed on the next page.

4   Type your access token code into the box provided.

5   Follow the step-by-step instructions on the screen to help you register and log-in.

6   You can now use your *Skillful* Digibook.

Your access token code only allows one user to log in, so don't give yours away, and make sure you use it within one year!